ESSENTIAL
LEADERSHIP
LESSONS

from the

THIN BLUE LINE

ESSENTIAL LEADERSHIP LESSONS

from the

THIN BLUE LINE

DEAN CRISP

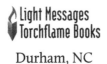
Light Messages
Torchflame Books

Durham, NC

Published 2021, by Torchflame Books
    an Imprint of Light Messages Publishing
www.lightmessages.com
Durham, NC 27713 USA
SAN: 920-9298

Paperback ISBN: 978-1-61153-379-8
Hardcover ISBN: 978-1-61153-380-4
Ebook ISBN: 978-1-61153-444-3
Library of Congress Control Number: 2020925284

To
Kim, Adam, and Andrew

CONTENTS

FOREWORD

By developing skilled and enlightened leaders, every organization can achieve extraordinary results. This book was developed the hard way, in the real world, by a results-oriented leader who has faced guns, bombs, dope fiends, riots, disgruntled employees, political espionage, lawsuits, mediocrity, and miracles. The author is a retired police chief who has worked, trained and taught throughout this nation and around the world. As a cop, he understands what it means to achieve the mission in the face of danger and controversy. Dean Crisp has learned just how essential it is to win the hearts and minds of human beings in order to accomplish the goals of an organization.

In this book, the author brings together academic theories of behavioral science, painful memories, emotional scar tissue, significant victories, and gut-wrenching breakthroughs. The sole intention of this book is to make other leaders more successful, and literally, have each reader benefit from Crisp's experience and lifelong pursuit of leadership knowledge. This book irreverently cuts through layers of complex language and research. It blasts through bureaucracy and distills the simple, compelling competencies that are essential to leadership success. These competencies will yield transformational results in every leader and every organization willing to learn, internalize, and apply them.

The competencies are the irrefutable knowledge, skills, and abilities that ensure consummate connectivity with people and superior business results. These competencies are a clear, distinguishable set of measurable wisdom and personal savvy. All have been hard-earned, but made available to you for the asking. Each of the competencies is quintessential to personal development and achievement of key objectives. The competencies are easy to remember. They provide a virtual roadmap to helping each leader become all he or she can be.

The police perspective is unavoidable, but beneficial. With over thirty years of experience, the author has survived both life-threatening and career-threatening scenarios. He studies hard, reads voraciously, and teaches leadership enthusiastically. But unlike many authors, he still practices and executes these competencies in the trenches, where both the mission and the people really count.

—Kathleen Sheehan, retired chief of police and
creator of the West Point Leadership Program

PREFACE

My motive and intent in writing this book is simple: I want to share leadership lessons and experiences which I hope will help you to become a better leader, and more importantly, a better person.

Over the past thirty years, I have learned that leadership must become a lifestyle, and that true leaders are always learning. I hope others can learn from my mistakes, my experiences, my education, research, observations, and reflections. I have experienced more than my share of failures, with a fair number of successes, and I have had amazing opportunities to learn from other people. My goal in writing this book was to sift through my knowledge and experiences to share the most valuable in the hopes that they will be beneficial to others. My intention is to help you avoid many of the mistakes I have made, and to help you capitalize upon the successes so you can become a better leader.

Becoming a police chief at the age of thirty-three was personally rewarding, but at the same time, it was extremely challenging. I had great confidence in my abilities to do the job, but I was not well-equipped for the challenge of leading other people. In other words, I was probably a good cop, but my competency as a leader was limited. I am certain that many folks I had the honor of leading suffered because of my inexperience and lack of knowledge. Despite this, our team accomplished some amazing things. Looking back, we probably took the long route more often than not, simply because of my lack of leadership experience. I give full credit to the men and women who worked with me, for their ability to overcome my shortcomings as their appointed leader. Leadership, after all, does not require a certain rank, and the people I worked with proved that in a real way.

Since childhood, I have had a strong desire to help others. Feels like it is in my DNA. It's what gets me get up in the morning and keeps me going. I have a deep desire and passion to see other people succeed and be the best they can be, especially when it helps them reach their full potential as leaders.

I still want to continue to grow and reach my own personal potential. Writing this book has pushed my limits and has helped me recognize how I can continue to improve; I have still have a long way to go. This book is designed to give you the best and worst of my experiences, research, observations, education, and anything else I think is relevant so you can avoid some of the mistakes I made along the way.

Since writing my first book, I have certainly learned many more lessons. Some are enhancements of the lessons in this book, while others will be future writings. Perhaps the most profound one is the importance of self-reflection. If there is one aspect of my journey through writing this book, and my motivation for writing future books, it is the importance of reflecting regularly along your journey. I try to do this daily through leadership journaling. I journal what I read and think about leadership, as well as my own personal experiences as a leader of my own company.

Since leadership almost always involves interacting with and relating with other people, you will likely learn, as I did, that the biggest part of leadership is creating quality relationships with coworkers, colleagues, and subordinates. In focusing on developing those relationships, leaders will find that their job becomes easier. If your people know you, and that you know them and trust them to act appropriately in any given situation, you will begin to see their personal and professional leadership grow. As they grow, your leadership grows as well.

As I always say, the rent you pay as a leader are the leaders you help create. Every day, you are leaving a leadership legacy. Make sure it's the one by which you want to be remembered.

INTRODUCTION

THE BUSINESS OF LEADERSHIP

"As a leader, you must have the leadership want-to, and you must want to lead for the right reasons."

—Dean Crisp

When I wrote my first book book *Leadership Lessons*, the focus was exclusively on the personal leadership lessons I have learned throughout my career. My goal was to share those as my legacy to future leaders to help them avoid some of the hard lessons I had to learn. As with many projects, you begin to reflect on the writings, and as many things evolve, I began thinking about a practical process that I would use with mentees to guide them through the evolution of leadership as I see it. That is what this new book is—a roadmap to success. A pathway to becoming an intentional leader.

In fact, one of the first things I did after writing my first book was to create my signature class—Intentional Leadership: Leading With A Purpose. In that class, I take students on a journey of how to become an intentional leader. After all, we tend to put energy and effort into the things we focus on—that is the definition of intentionality.

The pathway to intentional leadership was an evolution of my concept of the GPS Moment—when you determine where you are in your leadership journey, and decide where you want to be. The pathway, like a GPS system in your car, is what connects the two.

This book offers a roadmap to success for those who choose to follow it. The book has three sections, organized in a way that new or experienced leaders can follow clearly. The first section, "Leading Yourself," is all about the principles that help you begin to lead your own path. I believe that if you cannot lead yourself, you cannot lead others.

Learning the principles and techniques that help you lead yourself begin with understanding yourself at the base. Who are you? What are your values? Who has influenced you? What does your personality add or hinder you in your leadership journey? How emotionally intelligent are you? Why do you want to lead? What is your *why* of leading?

All of these are key elements in becoming more self-aware. The more self-aware you are, the more likely you are to be able to control yourself in key situations, and have a greater chance at influencing others. Influence is the number one key to leadership. Your ability to influence others through motivation and intrinsic action is considered the mark of the most effective leaders. In other words, our best leaders get us to act because we want to act for the organization, not because we have to do so.

In this section, I will walk you through some of the lessons I learned about leading myself, and I will offer techniques and tips that I found particularly helpful in growing as a leader. My hope is that the book will serve as both inspiration and a reference guide when you most need it.

The second section is all about leading others. In some ways, there may seem to be an overlap between leading the organization and leading others. But I want to be clear about the distinction. When you lead others, it is all about the legacy that you are leaving. My motto is that the rent you pay as a leader are the leaders you help create. What did you do to grow future leaders? Did you create passion? Did you show a clear mission? Did you mentor others? Most of all, did you show empathy?

As leaders, we have to understand that the potential we see in others is often not what they see in themselves. Conversely, we as leaders must guard against labeling a troubled employee as incapable of change. The empathy we show others is what makes or breaks the growth those employees experience. Remember, every person that works for you has a personal purpose. Your goal as a leader is to understand that purpose and help that employee live it. If they are living it, then they are in there power place, where they are self-motivated to become their best, every day.

Leading others means understanding the role emotional intelligence plays in your growth as a leader, and in how you can help others grow. The great thing about emotional intelligence is that it is the one aspect of a person that can evolve as long as they are self-aware of their own potential pitfalls, and as long as you as a leader are helping them grow in those areas.

Finally, the third section of the book is "Leading the Organization." This could be second or third, but I put it last because, as part of the leadership journey, office and social politics that occur within an organization can be the biggest barrier to your continued growth and influence as a leader. That said, you must understand that organizations are people. Understanding how to lead others effectively allows you to have greater influence on the organization, and hopefully, possess a better understanding of how to navigate the inevitable intraoffice and organizational turf battles we all face.

Leading organizations begins with understanding your people. When you become a leader, you are leading other people. They are at the core of what you do every day. Successful leaders learn early on how to place people at the core of their strategies, and how to communicate that message effectively. Organizational culture is typically what sets acceptable behaviors and perceptions of what is going on within the organization. How you manage the various factions (and every organization has them) within your organization can make or break you as a leader. I will walk you through my Diamond Leadership Model, which will be the goal of every leader to achieve lasting success.

Components of Successful Leadership

C2020 Crisp Consulting Group

Together, these three sections serve as a guide for today's 21st century leaders. As the Boomer and X Generations begin to retire, the Millennials and iGens will need guidance.

In many ways, they are well-suited to the challenges of the 21st century organization. Today's leaders must be holistic thinkers and have a growth mindset. The technology with which these two generations have been raised create a fundamental trend toward holistic thinking—seeing the big picture and having a growth mindset. Our goal is to nurture that natural tendency and offer leadership in areas where they may be lacking.

As overprotected children, many of today's younger professionals lack the basics of independent decision-making. That is on us. Our goal as leaders must be to help them attain those skills. As Boomers and Xers age out of the workforce, it is incumbent on those leaders to share the organizational and institutional knowledge with their younger successors.

These are all fascinating and exciting challenges for the growth-minded, optimistic leaders for whom I wrote this book. I hope it provides some new ideas to old leadership challenges, and serves as an ongoing reference manual for you as you grow your leadership skills.

I

LEADING
YOURSELF

It is impossible to lead others with any degree of success without first being able to lead yourself. When I first became a leader, I had this illusionary mindset of how simple and easy leading would be: I would give the orders, provide a little feedback, and people would instantly follow. It didn't take long to discover how naive that mindset was. I quickly understood that people may do what you say because you are in a leadership role, but the quality and effort they give is a direct result of their belief in you.

Leaders must be able to inspire others. By leading yourself first, you inspire others. Marcus Aurelius, the Roman emperor and Stoic philosopher, discovered that one of the most important components of leading was to first lead yourself. He spent a great deal of time in writing and reflecting on his own shortcomings and mastering himself.

Dee Hock, the founder of the Visa credit card association, is quoted as saying, "If you look to lead, invest at least 40 percent of your time managing yourself."

Consistent, honest self-reflection is the key to leading others. Throughout my career, I have had the opportunity to lead hundreds of people in all types of situations—some of those simple, and some complex. Without question, my ability to lead myself was the key to any success I may have enjoyed.

Personal leadership growth is the key to growing others. If you don't grow yourself it is impossible to grow others. The more I grow as a leader the more I desire to grow others. See growth as good news. Everyone wants to share good news, share it with others. Personal growth unlocks your potential and the potential of others.

The best leader I have ever worked for taught me a lesson early in my career. When problems would arise, and a crisis surrounded us, he would take a moment and self-reflect to see if his actions or inactions had led to the situation, and what could he do to correct that before assigning blame to others. And when credit was due, he would assign that to others quickly. The best way I could describe his self-reflection ability, is that when problems arose, he looked in the mirror for blame. And when things went well, he looked out the window to give credit.

Here are some thoughts that I will cover in Section 1, Leading Yourself:

- **Lead and Grow yourself first**. Know what experience will help you, and understand what intellectual capital you lack.

- **Be honest with yourself, and begin to develop a plan**. Only if you know where you are can you map the path to where you want to be. Designing a winning strategy will certainly help you become an effective decision-maker. It means knowing what you need to know by reading and researching everything; developing a strategy based on what you have learned and what you know; and finally, executing the strategy by implementing what you know, and understanding that you will learn more by trial and error. The goal is to be strategic in developing your decision-making strategy so you get more trials by having fewer errors.

- **Take inventory of your skillset**. In order to decide the type of leader you want to be, you must develop the foundational components you already possess, and cultivate the ones you don't already possess. Foundational components are those specific and unique skills that make you who you are. Taking inventory of the skills you possess, as well as the ones you do not, are vital to developing a path to leadership success. Skills include who you are and what you can do. Examples of who you are include your personality traits, such as good listener, decisive, charismatic. What you can do would include job skills that make you unique, such as the ability to mediate disputes within and outside the workplace. Are you emotionally intelligent? Organizationally aware? People-aware? Task-focused? Each leadership role will be impacted by these. Also, how have the values you have developed influenced the development of these personality traits and skills?

In the following chapters, I share lessons I've learned which will help you understand the importance of leading yourself.

CHAPTER 1

LEADERSHIP IS A LIFESTYLE

*If your actions inspire others to dream more, learn more,
do more, and become more, you are a leader.*

—John Quincy Adams

Being a leader does not begin or end with a nine-to-five work assignment. Leadership is a lifestyle. It is a constant and encompassing responsibility that requires your continuous energy and expertise. Effective leaders find ways to correlate their everyday life experiences into leadership lessons.

Leaders must be able to learn from their experiences and apply them to their leadership. Leaders must continually seek better understanding of the people they lead, and continually learn about leadership. Leadership cannot be turned on and off. It must become an integral part of your life.

It is not easy to adopt a leadership lifestyle. It takes effort and commitment. It is not a revolution of the mind, but more of an evolution. The American Psychological Society offers recommendations on how to transition important things in our life from good intentions into a lifestyle. These can easily be transferred to leadership.

The APA suggests the following:

- **Make a plan that will stick.** In the case of leadership, begin formatting a path to understanding leadership

at a higher level. See yourself helping others become better people and leaders.

- **Start small.** Don't try to do too much. Slowly work yourself into correlating life experiences into leadership lessons. Look at leadership differently.
- **Change one behavior at a time.** Don't try to do everything at once. Begin reading more. Begin spending more time thinking and talking about leadership with others.
- **Involve others.** This creates buy-in. Help others, and allow others to help you.
- **Seek assistance.** Find someone to mentor, and find a mentor for yourself. There is nothing like mutual cooperation and assistance with any project.

Leaders must sacrifice a great deal of their personal life to effectively lead others. By adopting leadership as a lifestyle, you create an internal mark that is constantly being evaluated. This enables you to make leadership a central part of your life.

This became clear to me as a chief. Once leadership becomes an active part of your lifestyle, the learning and doing becomes easier. Remembering that leadership is a lifestyle helps to keep me focused on leading, and helps control my actions in a way that is beneficial to making good decisions, thus helping the organization and others.

Since my retirement, I have been traveling the country, teaching leadership for the FBI's Law Enforcement Executive Leadership Development Association (FBI-LEEDA). I have met many wonderful people in my travel, and I have crisscrossed this great nation, teaching and sharing life's lessons with law enforcement leaders of all ranks.

One night, when my energy level was particularly low after a long stretch of travels, I received this e-mail from a student who had been in a class in Wisconsin. The e-mail lifted my spirits, and I was humbled by his kind words.

With his permission, I share it with you:

Dean,

I want to thank you again for the learning experience you provided in Altoona, Wisconsin this week. I've attended many law enforcement trainings over the last ten years, and The 7 Habits was one of the best.

I also want to finish my Monday homework assignment and share my inspirational experience with you, even though I chose not to share it in class.

Today is the eighth anniversary of my father's passing. He was a career member of the military, retiring as a major. He loved the South, and after retirement, moved to Southern Alabama. Throughout his military career, Dad read books from, and attended courses created by, Dale Carnegie, Zig Ziglar, and Stephen Covey. He lived by their lessons and preached their theories to me and my siblings. I especially remember him trying to get me to understand that we are a product of our choices, not a product of our circumstances.

I never really *got it* until my father was diagnosed with Lou Gehrig's Disease (Amyotrophic Lateral Sclerosis). He was diagnosed in September of 2001, and died April 15, 2002. The disease progressed very quickly compared to most cases, and he went from teaching, working, and walking, to wheelchair bound, and eventually bedridden, in just a few short months. He lost his ability to walk, speak, swallow, and eventually breathe, right before our eyes.

I felt angry, sad, and helpless as I watched his body deteriorate. He had good days and bad days, but what I remember most about those seven months was his ability to stay positive.

A few weeks before he died, I was sitting next to his bed, holding his hand, and I started to cry. At this point, Dad needed a computer to communicate, and it took a lot of effort for him to do so. He asked me why I was crying, and I was surprised by his question, thinking it was pretty damn obvious. My father explained that his disease was outside of his circle of influence, and that crying, worrying, and being angry was not going to change the outcome. He told me that we are not products of our circumstances, and we have the ability to choose to be happy. He was choosing to spend the last few months of his life happy, despite the terrible things his body was going through.

Dad asked us not to have a funeral for him, but to have a celebration-of-life party instead. He spent his last few weeks telling jokes and laughing with family and his nurses. My dad's legacy has inspired me and motivated me to live The 7 Habits.

It was a privilege to be part of your class this week, Dean. Your enthusiasm for the subject of leadership, your personal experiences, and your Southern accent reminded me a lot of my dad. Thank you. I will recommend this training to others in my agency, and outside the field. I believe that it is all part of an important, life-changing philosophy.

Ryan Weber
Marathon County Sheriff's Department
Wausau, WI

This simple e-mail reinforced to me how living a lifestyle of leadership can truly impact others, and re-energized my reasons for doing what I do and how I do it. Because leadership is so difficult and requires so much, it is important to hold on to positive feedback as a reminder of the difference you are making in another's life. Gestures such as this one, from those you lead, serve as reinforcement that you are doing right by them. This is not necessary, but everyone, including leaders, need motivation to ensure you are on the right course.

Tips for Making Leadership a Lifestyle:

- **Establish a reading plan.** On our website, www.lhln.org, you can find the reader resources for this book, which are a list of books that have had the greatest influence on my leadership.

- **Buy a journal.** Find the style that works for you. I have a preferred type and find that it works best for me.

- **Start small.** Read for a set amount of time, daily. Maybe it's listening on Blinkist or Audible, or physically holding a book. Take notes on concepts that resonate with you based on your experience.

- **Decide where you are as a leader in each area of your life**. Write it in your journal. Remember, goals for helping others grow will automatically make you self-reflect on how you can help them achieve their goals.

CHAPTER 2

DECIDE WHAT TYPE OF LEADER YOU ARE

Don't follow where a path may lead. Go Instead where there is no path and no trail.

—Ralph Waldo Emerson

Becoming a good leader is difficult, and requires a great deal of effort and skill. It is a journey, not a destination. And that journey is fraught with many challenges.

No leader can begin their journey, or improve their ability to lead, until they decide what kind of leader they want to be. I have given much thought to the types of leaders I've encountered in my career, and I have had the opportunity to observe thousands.

Below, are my three leadership categories:

- **Survivalist Leaders** lack maturity (ability to see the bigger picture) and are completely focused on themselves. They view every incident and situation from an *I* perspective, and their response is based on how it best serves them. They limit their mindset to see only the basic elements of most situations, and are reactive. They rarely take on difficult tasks, and act only when necessary. They are too dependent on other leaders to give them advice and provide perspective. They are not risk-takers, and their personal growth is limited. Rarely do they see the big picture, and they offer a limited perspective when asked.

- **Successful Leaders** broaden their focus to see past their own interest and consider the interest of their team. They take a *we* approach, and do not require the help of others with the decision-making process. Their interest lies in the welfare and success of others, and they seek ways to ensure a good outcome based on the team's best interest. They are more independent and require less supervision than their survivalist counterparts. Their maturity level is high. Therefore, they often see the bigger picture in most situations.

- **Significant Leaders** leave a positive, lasting impact on everyone they encounter. Their maturity level is also high. Their focus is on *us*, which includes all members of the organization. This level of maturity is difficult to maintain because individual consideration becomes secondary. This type of leader is always looking for ways to grow personally, and they share that growth with others. Creating partnerships is one of their main objectives. It's no longer just about *me*, or even *us*, but *all of us*. Significant leaders are the leaders we remember.

Types of Leaders

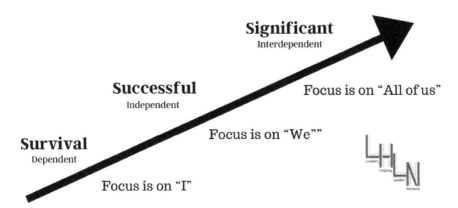

I've included this diagram to help you visualize leadership as a journey, and realize that even a survivalist leader can evolve to become a significant leader if they become self-aware and develop a growth strategy.

Determining the type of leader you want to be gives you a true north. It gives you direction and the focus necessary to guide you through your leadership journey.

Tips for Deciding the Type of Leader You Want to Be

- Take a values inventory, on our website www.lhln.org.
- Take our mindset inventory, at www.lhln.org.
- Make a list of your principles. Use leaders, both personally and professionally, who have impacted your thinking, and development of principles.
- Develop your *why* of leadership as it relates to your current leadership role and it's tie to the organizational purpose. (See my process for this in Reader Resources.)
- Develop a list your foundational competencies, and what is important to you.
- Create a list of strategies for your current leadership leader.
- Decide the type of leader you want to become.

CHAPTER 3

BE ALL IN

What our officers did yesterday was not their most heroic act. The day they embraced this profession, when they committed to a cause, and willingly accepted a life of risk and uncertainty to serve, that cause was their most heroic act. Every day after that was simply in the line of duty.

—A police chief
(at the funeral of two of his officers
killed in the line of duty)

When I'm teaching leaders across this great country, I often ask them, "Are you all in?" I first heard this from Dabo Swinney, head football coach at Clemson University.

In 2008, Coach Swinney was selected to follow Tommy Bowden at Clemson after a period of what some supporters of Clemson football would call the decline of the program. According to supporters, it was not merely a case of wins and losses. It was a question of toughness and total commitment to the program by players and coaches. In other words, before Coach Swinney arrived, the team didn't appear to be all in.

Immediately after taking over, Coach Swinney gathered his players and laid out his expectations for each of them. The coach emphasized what he wanted them to accomplish as individuals, and as a team, in the immediate future. Swinney ended his talk by asking each player if they were all in. According to reports, the coach received a resounding yes from every player. This began a new commitment to Clemson football, and a new day for the Tiger Nation. Coach Swinney's trademark of requiring each team member to be all in has taken hold.

Not only does Coach Swinney say it, he lives it. And I witnessed it. I have twin sons, and they are great baseball players. They played college baseball at the University of South Carolina. While attending a Clemson versus University of South Carolina baseball game during Coach Swinney's first year, I arrived early to watch batting practice.

Much to my delight, I saw Coach Dabo Swinney leaving the practice football fields, which were located close to a baseball stadium. I approached him and introduced myself. I told him about my sons playing baseball for South Carolina. After some good-hearted joking about Carolina beating Clemson on the baseball field that day, I asked him about how things were going as the new football coach at Clemson.

Coach Swinney's eyes lit up, and his demeanor changed. He replied, "This is the greatest opportunity in the world! Being the coach at Clemson means that our challenges are great, but with everyone being all in, we can't fail."

I was struck by Swinney's comments. I asked him to tell me more about the *all-in* idea, and how he could tell when someone was. He grinned real big and began explaining what it meant to him. The coach went on for a few minutes, describing just how vital this complete level of commitment is to the success of any endeavor.

During the 2015-2016 season, Clemson football, under the direction of Coach Swinney, was ranked number one in college football, and became National Champions. Obviously, his team was all in.

I instantly saw the applicability to any life challenge. The coach said that being *all in* means giving everything you have, no matter what you are faced with. No matter what the circumstances, you stay committed. I was struck by his enthusiasm and his passion for this idea.

We talked for a few more moments. I even asked Coach Swinney if he would speak to a friend of mine by telephone. The friend was a die-hard Clemson fan who, only a few weeks before, had been talking about how great this new coach, Dabo Swinney, was going to be for the team. The coach was cordial, and obliged my request. I have to admit, this certainly gained me much favor with my friend.

As Swinney hung up the phone, I thanked him profusely and told him how much I appreciated him taking the time to talk to me.

He said, "It's no problem."

His willingness to call my friend just further emphasized how being *all in* is a lifestyle for Swinney.

I think the coach really enjoyed our time together, even though I'm a Carolina fan.

As I walked away, I saw a number of small children running up to Coach Swinney. They asked him for his autograph and requested to have a picture taken with him. The coach gladly obliged. He playfully scooped up a few of the kids and held them off the ground for a minute or two. He looked each one of them in the eye and spoke with every child. I heard him ask them about themselves and how they were doing in school.

I was struck by that he didn't act as if he had to hustle away to attend to his team. The coach stayed outside the locker room until every one of the fans gathered had been given his full attention. Then it dawned on me: I had just witnessed what being all in was truly about.

The importance of being all in to you as a leader can be understood by examining your desired relationship with your children. As parents, we are expected to be all in, and we should be constantly on guard for what is best for our children. At a moment's notice, we will sprint to their side and aid them in any way possible. We never have to decide if we will protect them or help them; it is a given. And it is a good way to describe being all in. If your relationship with your children is not that great, substitute it with another example.

A few years after my encounter with Coach Swinney, I was watching one of his interviews. He was asked about the key to Clemson's success. Swinney smiled and said that every one of his players is assigned a task. They know what it is, and are given the tools to succeed. Then the most profound thing he said was, "It's up to them to bloom where they are planted."

Swinney's comment says it all. Great leaders assess their teams, know their strengths and weakness, as well as their capabilities, and help them bloom where they are planted. This is essential to successfully leading others.

In my career, when I am all in, I can clearly see a difference in the results of my efforts. Leadership comes from our commitment to seeing the task to completion. I do believe that failure is an option, because we all are going to fail. But the key is to understand that quitting is not an option, and being all in ensures this mindset. If you fall seven times get up eight.

Tips for Being All In

- Cultivate the right mindset.
- Gain a clear understanding of the end goal.
- Be comfortable with being uncomfortable.
- Don't take your eyes off of what you are trying to accomplish.
- See the bigger picture.

CHAPTER 4

MINDSET IS EVERYTHING

Anyone can train to be a gladiator.
What marks you out (makes you stand out)
is having the mindset of a champion.

—Manu Bennett

Mindset is one of the most important components of successful leaders. I am convinced that if you have the proper mindset, you will be a successful leader and experience change that endures. Conversely, if you set out to make a significant change in your life without changing your mindset, you will almost certainly fail and fall back into familiar, unsuccessful habits.

Mindset is defined by the *New World Dictionary* as "a fixed mental attitude or disposition that predetermines a person's responses to and interpretations of situations; an inclination or a habit."

I define mindset as your current state of mind, related to your expectations. Frankly, mindset is everything when it comes to having a successful career as a leader.

How we view the world matters. Everything we do, say, or think is directly affected by our mindset. Perhaps the easiest way to understand what I mean by is to look at the worst end of the spectrum—the people with an inherently negative outlook on life. Their mindset is negative. Therefore, they see just about everything from an ugly or depressing perspective.

All of us know such pessimistic people. Unfortunately, we probably know too many. Think for a moment how these negative people speak, think, and react. It seems like their entire attitude is beset by an unpleasant tone. Just being around people like that is usually draining, physically and emotionally. It is as if these naysayers suck all the positive energy out of every situation. Instead of looking forward to new challenges with a sense of wonder and curiosity, they fall back upon negative evaluations such as, *How much work will this be?*, and *I don't see a need to take on anything new.* You can hear the whining and grumbling in their voices. You can see it in their poor posture and facial expressions. My word, what a miserable way to live!

I used to work for a person who had a negative mindset. I tried to influence him to be positive, and help him view the world from a better perspective, but nothing seemed to work. He thought the worst of every situation, and to make matters even worse, he was vocal about his negative opinions. Our boss was so negative that it became disruptive to everyone. On a daily basis, his depressing personal editorials infected our entire worksite.

Soon, the downbeat view of the world became the norm. Most of our team was trapped in his cycle of negativity. As a result, we were caught in a rut. Our unit epitomized Albert Einstein's definition of insanity: doing the same thing over and over again, and expecting different results. We became one of the worst-performing units in the department. His mindset became ours.

Fixed Mindset vs. Growth Mindset

As I became more aware of how important mindset is to your effectiveness as a leader, I discovered that most of us tend toward either a fixed mindset, or a growth mindset. In order to convey this properly, let's discuss some of the differences of the two.

Stanford Professor Carol Dweck, in her landmark book *Mindset: The New Psychology of Success*, demonstrates, through her research, just how mindset impacts us, beginning at an early age.

Dweck explains that there are two types of mindsets that are prevalent in all of us:

- **Fixed Mindset**: The person with this mindset demonstrates a static way of looking at things, and usually shows an unwillingness to change. In children, you will see this in how easily they give up on a given task. They have learned to view the world from a cup half-empty view. In other words, they begin the cycle of negative self-talk with phrases such as, "I'm just not smart enough to that math problem," or "I just don't have the same physical skill that kid does." Many adults have experienced this when they have presented new ideas at work. While people are reluctant to change, a fixed mindset manifests in replies such as, "We can't do that," or "We have always done it this way." People with a fixed mindset typically see the world negatively, and view their ability to impact it as limited.

- **Growth Mindset**: This mindset, on the other hand, allows people to be flexible and see possibilities. Dweck's research shows that children with growth mindsets were typically encouraged to keep trying, by their parents or caregivers. These same growth-mindset-oriented children were more likely than their fixed-mindset peers to stick with a difficult task or math problem. Dweck found that these children's self-talk was much more positive, with phrases such as, "I just need to look at the problem differently," or "I will practice more, and I'll get the starting position." People with a growth mindset often embrace change and new ways to do things. They tend to look at problems as opportunities, and to encourage their employees to do the same. Having a growth mindset is key for leaders.

While many of us may have grown up with a fixed mindset, that doesn't mean we are doomed to stay that way. Often, just being aware of our fixed, or linear, way of looking at the world can help us realize what we are doing in any given situation, and adjust. Each of us has the ability to grow our mindset if we just become more self-aware. In a separate chapter, I will talk more about self-awareness as a key component of emotional intelligence.

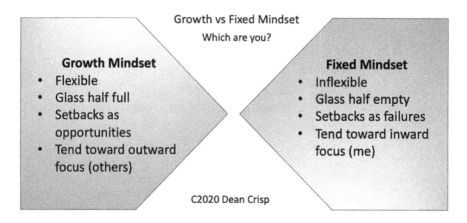

I must admit, I have not always had the best mindset. Late in my career, I discovered that my mindset was not as good as it should have been. This was pointed out not through self-discovery or by an employee, but by one of my sons, Andrew. It was Christmastime, and as usual, we were exchanging gifts with the family. I noticed that one of my gifts looked like a book. As I peeled the wrapping paper away, I found that it was indeed a book. But the title is what surprised me—*How to Be A Happy Father*.

I looked at Andrew, and he was smiling. I wasn't smiling.

I said, "Seriously?"

Andrew replied, "Yes, Dad, seriously! I love you, but sometimes you have a terrible mindset."

That took me by surprise.

"Dad, you never seem to be happy, and you're always on edge."

I knew he had a point.

Years and years of being a police officer and a chief of police had taken a toll on my mindset. I viewed the world from a negative mindset, and was allowing that to control me. I knew I had to make a change.

Andrew's gift led me to begin researching mindset. I read the landmark book written by Kevin Gilmartin, *Emotional Survival for Law Enforcement*. In it, Dr. Gilmartin discusses that paradigms and mindsets greatly influence our attitudes and actions, and that police officers in particular are overly sensitive to the events they encounter. This can cause major problems for them and their families. I realized that was living it.

In *The Seven Habits of Highly Effective People* by Stephen Covey, he defines our paradigms as the lens through which we view the world. My lens was definitely clouded with a negative perspective, and my mindset was a major contributing factor. I knew my first task was to change my mindset. I also knew it would not be easy to make such a major change. But that I had to do it. Andrew's gift had given me the awareness that I needed to see how I had become the person I used to dread. Mindset is the key to your paradigms.

Mindset is your current thoughts based on your expectations, and your paradigms provide the models or patterns for your thoughts. I had learned that mindset can greatly influence your paradigms. In other words, adjust your mindset, and your paradigms will follow. While there is so much more to mindset than simply breaking the shackles of negative behavior. Your mindset guides everything you do. How you view the world and how you approach life is a direct result of your mindset.

I remember, I was teaching a leadership class in Virginia, when a young officer came up to me at a break and said, "I really want to be a chief of police, but I don't think it will happen."

I was puzzled, especially since we had spent the last hour talking about how to become a better leader, and how to reach your full potential. So I asked the officer to explain.

He said, "I work in a small department of about twenty officers. My chief is relatively young, my captain is also young, and I just don't think I can wait them out."

I understood his point perfectly, but he was missing the bigger picture.

I said, "Have you ever thought that your mindset might be out of line with your goals?"

He looked surprised. "What do you mean?"

"The chief and the captain are not really your competition. You are your own competition."

I went on to explain that if he truly wanted to be a chief of police, the first order of business was to believe he could do it. Then he would begin to act responsibly, inspirationally, energetically, and to think as if he already had the position. I pointed out to this officer that if he desired to be a chief of police, there are thousands of small towns and big cities all over the country, and every one of them has a chief position. But he had absolutely no chance to land any one of those chief jobs if he did not see himself in the position.

This officer began our conversation thinking that other people were the obstacles that blocked his path to success. But after reflecting on what we discussed, he realized that he was his own obstacle.

Young officers like this one frequently come to me and ask for career advice. I recognize that giving advice is part of my responsibility as a leadership instructor and mentor, so I pay close attention. I try to phrase my advice in a personal way to meet the needs of the particular officer who is asking. This is what good leaders do. There is one gem of advice, however, that will benefit nearly everyone, in every field of endeavor: mindset is everything! With the right mindset, anything is possible. Without a strong and positive mindset, almost everything is impossible.

Whichever mindset you have—growth or fixed—is greatly affected by your time frame reference. The time frame reference is simply how far ahead you think. Time frame reference (short-term versus long-term) is often affected by growth versus fixed mindset. Fixed mindset leaders will often be so focused on results that they don't see the long-term impact. Whereas, those leaders with a growth mindset will be able to see the bigger picture and plan ahead for maximum success of their people and their organization.

Let me describe it with this illustration. Imagine sitting on a beach. Your mindset determines what you are looking at. Imagine you are looking at the beach chairs and the sand around your feet. This is a small view of the actual beach. This indicates a fixed mindset. Now expand your view into the water. You see the waves breaking, and people passing by. This is an example of an expanded mindset, but not a total growth one.

Now, look at the horizon. What do you see? Do imagine what is beyond what your vision? If you answer yes, then you are viewing life with a growth mindset.

What did early man see when he peered into the horizon? His mindset determined his vision and what he imagined as possible. Only with a growth mindset did we discover the earth was not flat.

There's a famous quote by inventor Thomas Edison that summarizes this whole point: "Many of life's failures are people who did not realize how close they were to success when they gave up."

Don't give up.

What time frame reference do you use? Does your mindset seek only immediate gratification? Or do you think ahead, drawing out a strategic plans to achieve your goals? Of course, even the best plans are subject to adaptation based upon changing circumstances.

A good leader has a growth mindset focused on long-term goals. Remember, this takes time and effort to develop—in yourself, and in those you lead.

Does your mindset include a healthy consideration of where you want to go and how to get there?

Tips for Having the Right Mindset

- Understand your mindset. Ask yourself, *Do I have a fixed or a growth mindset when faced with circumstances outside my comfort zone?*

- Realize the importance of how you view the world. It is paramount to realize you need to open your mind to new things.

- Become self-aware of how your mindset may be impacting your decisions, and work on having an open mind.

- Listen and see from the other person's point of view. Most of us don't listen, and we only see from our own perspective.

- Begin with the end in mind. If you can't visualize your future, you likely won't achieve it. Think about where you want to be, and when.

- Start slowly, with simple things. Such as, a choice of food that you may not have been open to in the past. Give it a try, and view it as a positive experience.

- Reduce your negative comments. Control your mind by controlling your tongue.

- Realize your impact on others. As a leader, you are the barometer of your organization. Your mood will set the tone for your people. Your mindset will as well. Be aware of this, and understand how it impacts your organization.

- Don't give up. When you think you have no new options, take a break, reflect, and then try again from a new perspective.

CHAPTER 5

LEADERS MUST BE COMMITTED

Anyone can hold the helm when the sea is calm.

—Publilius Syrus

True leaders understand that the ability to commit to something and to stick with it requires discipline and heart. It's an extension of keeping a promise. Sometimes what we promise requires grit, determination, and time. That's what separates a great leader from a mediocre one: following through on our commitments. After all, what is leadership but one big commitment to lead others through good times and bad?

I met a special person in Jackson, Mississippi, who epitomized commitment: a cab driver named Tommy Johnson. He was a man who lived up to his commitments in the purest and most remarkable sense.

At the time, I was working with a public safety group to sponsor a gang conference in Mississippi. I was facilitating the executive session, so everyone was relying upon me to arrive and get things started in a positive way—to set a strong tone for the entire conference. I had flown into Jackson from Atlanta, Georgia, on a rainy winter day. As most of us who travel frequently can attest, flights during stormy weather can be inconvenient at best, and sometimes dangerous. Fortunately, despite the storm, my flight had not been delayed. Other than a bumpy ride, the flight had been uneventful.

The hotel was about twenty miles away from the airport, and I needed transportation. I stepped out of the terminal and got slapped with an icy blast of wind. I was hoping that, even in this weather, there would be a taxi cab available. Fortunately, I spotted an older gentleman standing next to his cab. His name was Tommy Johnson. He was polite and helped me with my luggage and getting me settled in for the ride.

As I climbed into the backseat, Mr. Johnson peered at me through his thick, rain-drenched eyeglasses.

"Where are we going?"

I replied, "The Hilton Inn in Jackson. How much will that cost?"

"Around forty-two dollars and change."

"Okay, do you offer any discounts?"

Mr. Johnson chuckled. "If you can get the airport to give me one, I will pass it along to you."

We both laughed as he pulled out of the terminal. The conversation was minimal, and I checked my BlackBerry for text messages and e-mails during most of the trip toward the hotel. Even though the number of e-mails I get today is a far cry fewer than when I was a police chief, my messages still keep me busy.

Shortly after checking my messages, I placed a call to the FBI-LEEDA office. During my conversation, I inquired about the office manager, who had been out sick for a few days. I made mention that I would cancel my flowers to the mortuary in lieu of her returning to work. After a laugh from the other end, we ended the conversation, and I went back to looking at my phone.

Mr. Johnson said, "Do you have someone who is at the mortuary?"

It was obvious that he was concerned for me.

I replied, "Oh, no. I was just making small talk."

"Well, I hate to say this, but I do have someone at the mortuary right now."

36

"You have someone at the mortuary, today?"

"Yes. My wife of fifty-plus years died yesterday, and she is at the mortuary today."

"What in the world are you doing out in this weather, driving a cab today?"

"That was one of her wishes."

"Really!"

Mr. Johnson then went on to explain that just a few months back, his wife had been diagnosed with COPD, a lung disorder that can kill quickly. She had been to the doctor, who told her that because she had smoked for over fifty years, her lungs were not able to exchange oxygen correctly. Mrs. Johnson was slowly smothering because of the carbon dioxide buildup.

Mr. Johnson also mentioned that he had a daughter who had died in January of 2009, from the same disease his wife had suffered from. So, when the doctor made the diagnosis and told both Tommy and his wife that time was short, they believed him.

With a slight grin, Mr. Johnson said, "We figured we had about two more months together. We decided to make a list of things I was supposed to do when she passed. My wife always did have a list of *honey-do's* for me to accomplish. Well, one of the things on that list was for me to continue working. Keep on driving this cab. I have to honor her request, so that is what I am doing here today."

I was amazed at Mr. Johnson's commitment to his wife's wishes. I asked him whether it was hard for him to muster the strength to climb into the cab that morning, to start the engine, and get to work.

Mr. Johnson replied, "Mister, it was one the hardest things I have ever had to do."

He also shared that his wife had told him that she did not want him to shed any tears.

"She told me she would be waiting for me on the other side."

As the miles passed to the hotel, Mr. Johnson told me about his family and his commitment to them. He shared how deeply he loved his wife of fifty years, and how he had a son who was addicted to OxyContin. Mr. Johnson knew he would get an insurance check from his wife's death, and he had already vowed to spend every dime to get his son some help.

As we came to the end of our taxi ride and arrived at the hotel entrance, I could see a tear trickling down Tommy's wrinkled face, and I was sorry we didn't have longer to travel. The forty-two-dollar fare didn't seem like so much money, after all. I got out of the backseat and realized how lucky I had been to share a cab with Mr. Johnson, because I had just been in the presence of true commitment and love.

Mr. Johnson taught me an important lesson about commitment and leadership, whether in one's family, or one's job. Staying focused and determined to complete what you start will be a clear sign of your ability to lead. Don't falsely believe that others will not judge you by what you get done, or by what you leave undone. Staying committed to yourself, your mission, and core values will make a huge difference in how you lead others.

Learn from Mr. Johnson's commitment to his wife. Even under the most difficult circumstances, he stayed true to his word.

Tips on Being Committed

- Start with your personal commitments. If you cannot be committed to your family, spouse, or children, you will not be sincere in your professional commitments either. Promising to be home for dinner, or to play catch with your son after dinner are important to them and should be important to you. What you do in your personal life will impact your professional life.

- Start small. Make micro-commitments. If you are not sure you can do the whole promise, start with a smaller piece of it.

- Ask questions to clarify. Be sure you understand what type of commitment is being asked of you. Find out what the real issue is so you can address that, and not something on the fringe.

- Follow through. When you have made the commitment, follow through on it. If circumstances change that make it difficult to follow through, make sure to explain what has changed, and why you can no longer honor the commitment.

CHAPTER 6

BE WILLING TO PAY THE PRICE

If you are determined enough and willing to pay the price,
you can get it done.

—Mike Ditka

Leadership comes with a personal price, and you can't lead effectively if you aren't willing to pay it.

As I speak around the country, I spend time talking about the ability to accomplish great things, which I believe you can accomplish if you are determined, and willing to pay the price. But the personal cost can be substantial.

No, I do not mean a monetary price (not usually, anyway). Great achievements require a significant investment of ourselves. When I got serious about becoming a police chief, I had to take a personal inventory of my education, skills, abilities, and work experience. During this self-evaluation, I was employed at the Buncombe County Sheriff's Office in Asheville, North Carolina. I had been at the department for about four years and was ready to get back into municipal law enforcement. For those of you who may wonder what is different between municipal law enforcement and county law enforcement, the answer is, *a lot*. Most sheriffs' offices patrol the rural areas of a community and are responsible for a much larger geographical area. City police agencies take care of a more concentrated area, and focus on crimes in the city. The politics of the agencies are entirely different. This is especially true in the South because the sheriff is an elected official. He has almost unlimited power to hire and fire employees. Most, if not all, city agencies have more restrictions on the ability to hire and fire.

My educational pursuits were a great example of the willingness to pay the price. I attended college when you had to be physically present in the classroom to earn credit. Each week, I would sit in class for eight to ten hours at night. This necessary preparation took precious time from my home life and children, but I was willing to pay the price because I knew it would give me a better chance of being promoted to chief.

The same was true when I was hired by the United States Secret Service, and was given the assignment of Miami as my first duty station. I went through an arduous hiring process that lasted two years. When it finally came time to commit to taking the job, an agent who was hiring me said, "You have to make a choice. When you become an agent, you will experience some of the greatest career achievements, but be away from home a great deal. Or you can remain a local police officer and be at home most nights and coach your kid's baseball teams."

I knew that if I were to become a police chief, I was most likely going to have to move away from my community and home. My kids were little, and my wife was in the middle of finishing her nursing degree. Was I willing to ask my wife and children to pay the price of moving everyone, in my pursuit of becoming a chief? Anyone who has ever moved from their home community will tell you that it is tough to relocate and lose your support system and your familiarity with everyday conveniences. It is hard to start over and meet new friends.

After much deliberation, as a family, we determined that we were willing to pay the price, and it has worked out tremendously for us. My career pursuits were advanced by great measure. Moving to a different town, where I could be the chief, was one of the best decisions I have ever made. My family eventually joined me in my new town, and my true friends always visit no matter how much geographical distance is between us. Willingness to pay the price has paid off.

As a leader, sometimes you have to recognize that you're not always willing to pay to the price. Discernment is an important part of leadership. One instance for me came several years after I became a chief. I had often thought about going to law school and becoming an attorney. My career was successful, and life was good, but Father Time was tapping me on the shoulder, saying, *If you are ever going to be an attorney, time is running out.* I began looking at going to law school and starting a new career. I even took the LSAT and applied to several schools. When it came to decision time, I was not willing to pay the price to start over.

Leaders must understand the price can sometimes be extremely high. From time to time, I have been faced with a major decision, and had to add up the costs. Sometimes I decided that I was not willing to pay the price to move forward. Some may view this as weak, or as not being determined enough, but I disagree. Leaders make difficult choices all the time. Knowing what they're willing—and capable—of doing is as important as their commitment to doing it. It is better to know early what price you are willing to pay and what price you aren't. It will save you a great deal of time and energy.

I can remember when I was deciding to take the position of police chief in another state. This meant moving my family to a new location and starting life all over again - new home, friends, doctors, schools, grocery stores, basically a whole new life. Together, my family and I decided that we were not willing to pay the price this time. It was the best decision we could have made at the time.

Tips for Deciding Whether to Pay the Price

- Take inventory or your present situation.

- Assign a value to each item, keeping in mind that not all things are equal. For example, decisions that affect the family decisions outweigh a decision that affects only you.

- Be honest with yourself. Don't over- or under-value the impact of the cost.

- Avoid impulsive decisions.

- Remember the grass is NOT always greener on the other side.

CHAPTER 7

HAVE SELF-CONFIDENCE

If you have no confidence in self,
you are twice defeated in the race of life.

—Marcus Garvey

Having the self-confidence to lead is critical to being successful. In the movie *U-571*, the executive officer of an American submarine during World War II is played by Matthew McConaughey. The submarine, guided by the captain, is tasked with a cover mission to capture a German U-boat and confiscate a decoder being used by the Germans to intercept messages sent by the Allies. As fate would have it, the submarine that the executive officer is on is sank by a German submarine, and the captain is killed. The executive officer is now in charge, and he has to make a series of life-or-death decisions within moments of taking over the sub. The crew is looking to him for direction, hoping they will be saved.

The executive officer gives a series of orders, even though he himself seems to lack confidence in some of the directives he issued. The executive officer is questioned by one of the surviving members about the orders.

He replies, and I am paraphrasing, *Look, I don't have all the answers right now, but this is what we should do.*

The crew looked at each other, and the confidence drains from them. The salty old chief petty officer grimaces with obvious disbelief. He quickly takes charge and helps the captain-executive officer.

Shortly afterward, he has a private moment with the captain, and says, "With all due respect, sir. Don't ever show your lack of confidence in front of these men. They are depending on you to get us out of this. No matter what, you are the captain, a mighty and powerful person in the navy. Showing a lack of personal confidence will create doubt and maybe even fear."

Although we never want to be so overconfident that it appears we are arrogant—not willing to listen or learn—we must always show confidence in our own abilities. The trick is finding the balance. Always be aware that there is a razor-thin line between arrogance and confidence. Expressing a quiet confidence is paramount to leadership success.

In *Strengths Based Leadership* by Barry Conchie and Tom Rath, the authors found that people with higher self-confidence often end up with much higher incomes than people with lower self-confidence. Another interesting fact the authors found is that people with higher self-confidence had fewer health problems. Strikingly, people with lower self-confidence had three times as many health-related problems compared to their more confident compatriots.

Because I have been competitive most of my life, I have used that natural drive to boost my confidence. It is easy to have confidence when you have natural talents or skills, as I did early in my baseball career. But if you lack skills and a competitive drive, you have to dig deep to find the confidence necessary to succeed.

An example early in my career was my desire to be good at public speaking. I did not have any confidence in this area, due to an experience I had in the sixth grade that made me so afraid of public speaking I vowed that I would avoid it at all costs. I was running for student council representative and had to give a speech in front of the entire sixth, seventh and eighth grade. The auditorium was full, and each candidate had five minutes to give the reason why others should vote for them. When it came my turn, I had my remarks ready. I stepped to the stage, looked out into the audience...and froze. I can still feel the panic and desire to run in the pit of my stomach. Somehow I made a few remarks, but nowhere near my entire speech, and sat down before I passed out. That crushed my confidence in speaking in public, and impacted me for years.

When I became a police officer, drugs were rampant on the streets and in high schools. I knew I could help students if I could find a way to talk to them and tell them about the destruction drugs could cause in their lives. I wanted to make presentations to high school students on the perils of using drugs, but I was terrified of speaking to groups, and I knew I had to develop the confidence to speak in public. So I started slow and began speaking to small groups, then increased to a classroom size—all the while, building my self-confidence. I even bought a video camera to tape myself while making presentations. This was no small expense in 1980. Video cameras where the size of news cameras, and cost me $3,000. I had to make payments for four years on that equipment. But I slowly gained confidence and improved my public speaking skills. It wasn't long before I was making presentations to entire schools. A major accomplishment for me, since the last time I did that I almost fainted.

Tips to Help You Achieve Self-Confidence

- Envision where you want to be.
- Be willing to face your fears.
- Be willing to work at your weaknesses.
- Believe in what you are doing. If you believe, others will also.
- Stay focused. Don't let failure deter your success.

- Practice self-confidence in settings that will ensure success. Take small steps toward building your confidence.

- Be aware of your self-talk. Awareness of how you speak to yourself makes a difference. If you think you can, or you think you can't, you are right.

CHAPTER 8

SETTING YOUR PERSONAL GPS

A leader takes people where they want to go.
A great leader takes people where they
don't necessarily want to go, but ought to be.

—Rosalynn Carter

Are you on the right road? Does your mental map have you headed in the right direction? Do you know where you want to be?

Most of us don't. We go through life with someone other than ourselves determining where we are going and how we are going to get there.

Think about it: Do you know where you are going? To know where you are going, you must first know where you are, because understanding your present position in life is paramount. This is what I call a GPS moment. Just as the global positioning system (GPS) can pinpoint your exact location at any time, you must connect to your internal GPS and define your current location.

At times, when in a shopping mall, I've had to use the store directory. I recall a moment when I was standing at a mall directory, looking for the location of a particular ice cream shop. After scanning the map, I soon found what I was looking for. But to reach any destination, you have to first know where you are starting from. So I looked to see how far away that ice cream shop was from my current location, and I noticed that familiar big red star with the arrow and *You are here* beside it. Now this certainly wasn't the first time I had seen this, but it suddenly had a big influence on me. I paused for a moment and thought, *This is physically where I am in the mall, but could this also be metaphorically where I am in life?*

This situation became a defining moment for me. I realized that the star on the map was an indicator of exactly where I was at that moment. But symbolically, it also represented where I was in the pursuit of my life's journey, and it made me think, *Do I really know my present location and where I'm going in life?*

That moment helped me to evaluate and begin to recognize the importance of knowing exactly where I was in life. I know that it sounds crazy, that simply by looking for a store in the mall, you would see a red star and contemplate life's deepest meanings. But that is exactly what happened. It also reinforces how important it is to live leadership as a lifestyle, as stated earlier. If I was not attuned to leading myself, the lesson would have passed and never had the impact it did.

The story *Alice's Adventures in Wonderland* by Lewis Carroll, contains a wonderful example of how Alice experienced a GPS moment that changed her journey. Most of us are familiar with the story of Alice falling into the rabbit hole and entering a world beyond imagination (although crafted from her own imagination). As Alice traveled through this Wonderland, she got lost. Fortunately, she happened upon the Cheshire cat and asked him for directions.

Their encounter went like this:

> Alice: Would you tell me, please, which way I ought to go?
>
> Cheshire Cat: That depends a good deal on where you want to get to.
>
> Alice: I don't much care where.
>
> Cheshire Cat: Then it doesn't matter which way you go.

The cat was right. If you do not know where you want to go, then any road will suffice. Dare we trust our entire futures to such happenstance?

Yes, many of us live in precisely that way. We wake up every day without a clear idea of where we are or where we are going. Too often, we fail to understand that the road that we are on may be a dead end. We mistakenly allow others to provide our direction. We allow others to determine our future by failing to take control of our own lives.

In *The 7 Habits of Highly Effective People*, Stephen R. Covey writes that having a clearly defined mission statement gives direction and guidance in your life. If you were to ask yourself where are you going, or even what is your life's mission, could you answer? Do you let others influence and design your life, then complain about where the road ultimately takes you? I learned early in life, and in my career, that if you do not take a direct role in determining your future, others will provide the direction for you. Live without clear goals, and other people will determine your destination.

As a police chief, I was speaking with a group of employees about the direction we were headed as an organization. I compared the organization to a bus that we were all riding in down the highway of life. I asked everyone to imagine the bus, and told them, "Which seat are you occupying on this bus? Some seats are up front. Some are in the middle, and some are in the back. Some seats are near the bathroom. Some have a great view, and some are right next to the driver. Which seat are you in?"

I got puzzled looks from some folks, and nods from others.

Then I followed up with, "Who determines where you sit?"

"You do, Chief," said one employee.

I looked directly at that person. "I certainly hope not."

You should have seen the confused looks I got from some of the men and women present.

"I don't determine where you sit on the bus. You determine where you sit. When you decide you don't like your seat, then you do the things necessary to change seats."

They understood then that they were their own driver, and in charge of their own destiny, as long as they took control of their lives.

GPS moments are a starting point. From there, you follow-up with a definitive plan to get where you want to go. Having a definitive GPS moment is the cornerstone to defining your course in life. No one ever gets in the driver seat of their car and starts the engine without a clear understanding of where they are and where they are going. Why do that with your life?

Tips For Finding Your GPS Moment

- Take a moment and ask yourself, "Where am I personally and professionally?"

- Once you've defined where you are, ask yourself, "Where do I want to be?"

- Make sure that, just like your mobile GPS device, you are getting a clear signal. Don't be overly influenced by emotion.

- Take a self-reflective inventory.

CHAPTER 9

TRUST YOUR INSTINCTS

When you have a dream that you can't let go of,
trust your instincts and pursue it. But remember:
Real dreams take work, they take patience,
and sometimes they require you to dig down very deep.
Be sure you're willing to do that.

—Harvey Mackay

Trusting your instincts as a leader is invaluable. Developing those instincts can take many years. You will encounter countless people who do not have you or your company's best interest at heart. They are manipulative, and may appear to be well-intentioned, but in reality they are only thinking of themselves. I understand this may seem to conflict with what I have said about partnering with employees and working with them. I truly believe this is the best avenue for success. But as a leader, we must also be aware of those who seek to do harm.

I can remember when a career criminal and cagey character manipulated a number of us into believing that he was going to cooperate with us. He was in our Jail for murder. Roy Fox was a notorious serial killer. By the time he reached his fifties, he had spent most of his life in prison for murder. Fox had been paroled in Texas a few earlier after helping authorities gather testimonial evidence from a fellow inmate which resulted in the murder conviction of another inmate whom both Fox and the other inmate had known while serving time. I never understood how any prison system could have allowed the release of Roy Fox, but such is the injustices of our justice system.

Shortly after his release, Fox committed yet another murder in Buncombe County, North Carolina. He shot a man in cold blood after having a few drinks with him. After Fox killed the victim, he placed the man's body in a drainage ditch. Fox was also a suspect in several other murders at the time.

Roy Fox truly seemed devoid of any conscience. He was notorious for his ability to talk with people and convince them of just about anything. I wonder how many people had met their demise by his hand.

Fox was being held in the Buncombe County jail until his trial for the murder of the man he discarded in the drainage ditch. I was a captain at the time and in charge of that jail. As I said, Fox was cagey. He devised a plan to help himself by providing us information on an unsolved murder of a young couple that had occurred a few years before at Buzzard's Rock, a popular mountain overlook in Asheville, North Carolina. As you can imagine, this double murder had generated a great deal of news coverage, and rightfully so. It had officers looking for any help that may solve the crime.

Fox understood fully how to manipulate anything to his advantage. That the case had never been solved created an opportunity for Fox to negotiate a deal. After all, this kind of deal had resulted in Fox's freedom on a prior occasion. He saw no reason it wouldn't work again.

Roy Fox convinced the sheriff, Buck Lyda, that he knew who had killed the young couple. Fox also claimed that he knew where the murder weapon was located. Fox told the sheriff that he could not accurately describe where the gun was, but that he could show him the spot. The sheriff instructed our SWAT team to prepare a plan to take Roy Fox out of jail and transport him to the place he claimed the weapon was located.

In addition to being in charge of the jail, I was the commander of the SWAT team. Our team leader, Sergeant Tony Coggiola, prepared the tactical plan. It was a wintry day when we transported Roy Fox out of the jail.

Needless to say, we were cautious with him, and most of us thought he was up to no good. So our instincts were on high alert. We thought he was likely planning some type of escape, and we came prepared with plenty of personnel and weapons.

Fox led us on an all-day wild-goose chase. We went into the mountains and stopped in several places. Each time, we got out of the cars and took Fox into the woods under close guard.

Fox would point out a particular spot and say, "Look under that log right there."

We would dig and look, but we found nothing. I remember the sheriff falling for Fox's antics by actually digging with his bare hands under a big log, and I thought, *This guy is such a con artist. He's convinced us that he's trying to help us. All the while, he's enjoying watching us run around in the mountains like children on an Easter egg hunt.*

After about the third stop, it was obvious what Roy Fox was doing. Fox was not looking for a murder weapon; he was looking for any opportunity where we would let our guard down so he could escape.

We loaded him back into the car and headed home. We were tired and aggravated, but Fox's plot had only limited success.

He continued his antics in the weeks to follow. Shortly after that outdoor adventure, Fox tried to break out of jail. He forged a handgun out of paper magazines and tried to bluff his way out by threatening a jailer's life. Thank God the jailer did a great job by slamming Fox's cell door shut before he was able to convince the jailer that he would shoot him. We had a standoff with Fox that lasted about an hour. He stayed in the locked cell with what we believed to be a handgun. We were all convinced that, somehow Fox had managed to get a gun into the jail.

Eventually, Fox realized his situation was hopeless, and that he had no chance of escape. No one was in a vulnerable position to be shot. So even if Fox did have a gun, he was clearly going to remain in jail.

At last, Fox threw the gun out of the cell. After securing him, we examined the gun and learned it was not real. We all were amazed at the intricate detail of Fox's pseudo-weapon. It looked just like a revolver. He had spent days planning and preparing his attempted escape, all to no avail. Somewhere deep inside, Fox must have thought he was a modern-day John Dillinger.

In dealing with this career criminal, we all learned a valuable lesson. We had always known that dealing with Roy Fox was risky, but we were convinced that the payoff would be worth it. We all trusted our instincts and were well-prepared for what may have come.

Manipulators often convince us that what they offer is worthy of the risk we will take. As evidenced by just about everything Fox did, from negotiating with Texas authorities, to running us on a wild-goose chase, to fashioning a gun out of paper, he was simply a phony.

Trusting your instincts is a primal responsibility that requires a connection between knowledge, experience, and judgment. Listen to your instincts. They may save your life.

Tips For Learning to Trust Your Instincts

- Listen to your inner self.
- Be aware of the physical sensations you receive.
- Journal your experiences.
- While not always 100 percent correct, intuition is enough to make you look twice.
- Don't overthink, but at the same time don't under-think.
- Intuition is a gift from your soul. Open it with care.

CHAPTER 10

SET PERSONAL
AND PROFESSIONAL GOALS

The task of the leader is to get his people from where they are to where they have not been.

—Henry A. Kissinger

Over the past several decades, most of us have heard how important it is to set goals. Many organizations, leaders, and authors tout the importance of setting goals, which provide vision and direction. But despite the benefits of setting goals, most of us still have not done so. Yes, that's right—*we have not set goals, despite knowing we should.*

I have seen many strategies for setting goals. Some state it that is ideal to do so with one-year, three-year, and five-year timelines. Another strategy is to divide goals into immediate, intermediate, and long-term goals. No matter what the preference, the core message is important: setting goals will improve your life. It's that simple.

Once you set your goals, determining a strategy to achieve each one is vital. Remember, a goal without a strategy is only a wish, with little chance of coming true. So after I set personal and business goals, I develop specific strategies to achieve them.

Your strategies must be within your tactical and technical skill levels. *Tactical skills* are abilities that are within your physical realm of possibilities. For example, setting a goal to become an NFL player while never having played football. You may want to play in the NFL, but you would certainly lack the tactical skills.

Technical skills are your cognitive abilities. For example, wanting to become an IT expert without knowing anything about a computer. You would lack the knowledge to do your job.

The importance of a strategy cannot be overstated. A goal without a strategy is simply a wish. Wishing that something positive will happen is good self-talk, but it does little to help you move forward.

I have also tried to teach my sons the importance of setting goals. From the time they were little boys in grade school, I required both of them to write down their goals for each year, along with a description of how they were going to accomplish each endeavor. I encouraged the boys to place the goals in a visible place so they could be reminded of the things they wanted to do, and how they intended to accomplish them. My sons would comply, but I could tell that they wrote down goals and strategies mostly to please me, rather than from a heartfelt desire to achieve them. Despite my encouragement, their efforts were half-hearted, which was understandable.

About the time they were to graduate from college, we had a candid conversation about their lack of achievement and genuine goal setting. They were the ones who brought up the subject, and were open about their failure to achieve some of their goals. They both said that they felt they had fallen way short on accomplishing some important things in their career, and with life in general. They went as far to say that their life would be much more successful if only they had taken goal setting and strategy more seriously.

Adam said, "Dad, if I had really listened to you when you made me write down my goals and place them all over the house, college would have been a heck of a lot easier. We used to think that was a pretty silly exercise, but now we realize that it would have made a big difference for us if we had paid attention, made a plan, and seen it through. For one thing, we probably would have graduated college in three years instead of five. It certainly would have been a heck of a lot less expensive, and we would not have to repay all these big student loans we have now."

My wife and I looked at each other and smiled.

"Why didn't you make me listen better?"

Kim and I assured him that he was still a young man and still had several years ahead of him to become better at setting and achieving goals. We also congratulated both of them on figuring it out when they did. Because even if it did take five expensive years of college, the truth is that both had discovered a fundamental principle of success—set goals and see them through!

Both have since graduated college, and the importance of goals has changed. Setting goals is no longer a mandate from me; it has become a way for them to accomplish higher levels of achievement.

Over the course of my career, I also had numerous moments to recognize the importance of setting goals and achieving them. Shortly after being appointed chief of police in the city of Greer, South Carolina, I recognized that the organization had few stated goals. I asked several Greer employees what their direction for the future was, or where they were headed in life. Most often, I would get blank stares and mumbled comments. The police department, in particular, was suffering from low morale. It had no clear direction, and no unifying goals or strategies.

I was new at being a chief, but I knew that in order to move forward, we needed some direction and goals. How could we accomplish anything if we did not know what we were going after? In the short term, I set some small but achievable objectives. Once the staff saw our mutual success, it was easier to build them up to bigger challenges. Shortly after my first year in Greer, I knew it was time, and my people were ready for more formal, long-term goal setting for the police department.

I had researched strategic planning and goal setting in college, and was familiar with the basic tenets. The trick was how to integrate these complex methods into a small-town police department, in a way that got everyone to participate and enjoy the process.

It occurred to me that the best way to get this started would be by holding an offsite retreat for all my supervisors. I believed that we should leave the daily work behind and meet in a pleasant setting in the mountains. My hope was that everyone would relax and be willing to freely exchange their best ideas so we could get collaboration and buy-in from all the supervisors.

I selected Asheville, North Carolina as the location. It was only about an hour from our city of Greer, and it offered a bucolic setting. By going an hour away, we could get away from the distractions of everyday responsibilities, but still be available to respond in case of a major emergency.

The retreat began on Friday morning, with a nice drive. We divided up driving responsibilities, and paired who rode with whom according to each supervisor's job assignment. I mixed patrol sergeants with detective supervisors, for example, just to give every employee a chance to converse with someone from outside their daily contacts.

Because I am originally from Asheville, I had friends and contacts in that city. Coincidentally, a good friend of mine was the general manager of a Courtyard by Marriott hotel. So he gave us a great rate, which allowed us to stay three days and two nights. My friend also included the meeting space at no extra charge, so there was no need to do any more commuting.

As people started arriving, we assigned the attendees to their rooms. This time, I made it a point to put direct coworkers together. For example, if you worked with a supervisor with the same squad, you were now roommates for the duration of the retreat. This worked well. It appeared that people who roomed together bonded better, and I would end up with more cohesive shifts in the long run.

We began our work that very day. The first and most important part of the retreat was to get everyone on the same page. We accomplished this with a training class on strategic planning and goal setting. It was a good first day, and it seemed as if everyone understood why and what we were trying to accomplish.

We began again bright and early Saturday morning. We recapped the previous day's training and began discussing how strategic planning and goal setting related to us as an organization. Next, we discussed where we wanted to go and how were we supposed to get there.

The discussion was candid, especially when I pressed them to identify some specific goals and how we would accomplish them. I soon realized that this was the first time many of them had openly discussed the future of the police department. They seemed to be unorganized, which I had expected as a stage we could work through.

One brash sergeant who was likely prompted by his peers, blurted out, "You know, Chief, this stuff sounds good, and it may work in some places. But why do you believe that our little department at Greer can do half the stuff that needs to be done for our people? How are we going to get any police officer to believe that we can make this happen?"

It was not a shock to hear this skepticism. To be honest, I had expected much more.

I replied, "Have you ever thought it possible to make this police organization the best in the state?"

The sergeant looked surprised. "Not really."

"Why not?"

"Because around here, we are just trying to be the best in the city."

His comment was revealing, and brimming with not-so-subtle sarcasm (the Greer PD was the only police department in the city of Greer!). I knew, though, that he had made a real point. That gruff, unpolished sergeant spoke the perspective of nearly everyone in the room.

Because lack of planning and goal setting was the norm, this organization had accepted a culture of mediocrity. We were unable to progress beyond our supervisors' perceived limits. Clearly, this attitude was a major hurdle to moving forward. Something had to change, and I was in the room with the people I needed to help me make that change.

The remaining time was filled with a great deal of open communication and candid comments. We left the retreat on Sunday with only a few specific goals and objectives for the next year. But a few were better than nothing, and I was certain that the seeds of change had been sown. We all had a clear understanding that this was a great start, and that planning and goal setting would play a major role in our organization in the future.

Over the next thirteen years, we held a retreat every year. What began as a simple goal-setting session became a major part of the growth and development of our entire organization. People felt that their opinions and ideas mattered, and that their suggestions were considered and acted upon.

The first retreat was the foundation, and we progressed to include the entire department in our planning and retreat process. The last year I served as chief, we had accomplished over eighty significant goals.

Goals are important. But more significant are the strategies you develop to accomplish them.

Tips for Setting Goals

- Set obtainable goals. Goals within your technical and tactical skill set. Setting goals that are outside of these skills can lead to early failures and decreased success.

- Set *through* goals, not *to* goals. This may sound strange, but I found that if you set a goal to something, when you reach it, you will stop. If you set a goal through it, you will work past the goal. For example, if you want to lose weight, don't set a pound limit. Set the goal to eat healthy and exercise.

- A goal without a strategy is a wish. Make sure your goals always have a clear strategy. The more definable, the more likely you will reach it.

- Set strategies that have short-term success. Success will breed success.

- Set goals that match your technical and tactical skill set. Setting goals too far outside of one's abilities and skills can lead to early failures and decrease one's success.]

CHAPTER 11

ENJOY EVERY DAY AND
SEE LIFE AS A JOURNEY

*The best gift we can have is living in the present moment
and really enjoying it for what it is.*

—Amy Smart

Most of us are too busy with life to enjoy it. We do not take the
time to relish the joys of each day. We are so focused on problems,
tasks, and the usual daily grind that enjoying the moment seems
impossible.

I have discovered that most leaders don't take the time to stop
and enjoy the fortunes of the day. They are more interested in
getting ready for tomorrow. This can cloud our appreciation of
today, and ultimately damage our ability to truly enjoy life's simple
pleasures, or the journey. We are caught up in the hustle and
bustle of daily responsibilities that make our lives less enjoyable.

Whenever I travel to Salt Lake City—which is not enough—I
am always struck by the majestic mountains and beautiful scenery.
Many of us live in scenic places, but few can match Salt Lake.

During the first few moments of a recent class there, I asked
the students, "On the way to class today, did you stop to notice
the beautiful surroundings? Do you stop and notice them every
day?"

I was quite surprised when most answered no. A few students who had lived in the Salt Lake area their entire lives even asked me, "What is so special about Salt Lake?"

Being successful as a leader can be difficult. Success is not guaranteed simply because you hold a position of rank or authority. Leadership is a journey of daily interactions, decisions, and hard work. It is full of highs and lows, with many trials and tribulations that mold and shape you as a leader. Enjoying the journey is important. Yes, even the low points. I have found that my low points, as tough as they were when I was experiencing them, taught me much. With a self-evaluative mindset, I have realized that leadership is not a destination, but is truly a journey.

Part of being an effective leader is knowing that you will never reach a pinnacle where you can say, *I have arrived*. Every day, we face difficult, complex situations, and around each corner, we find yet another challenge. Your leadership trek is never-ending.

During my twenty-one years as the leader of a police organization, I was constantly aware that I was on a journey. Unfortunately, I often focused on the quest for tomorrow instead of the richness and lessons of today. My mindset was to achieve my goals at all costs, to boldly charge forward toward pending projects and incessant objectives. Now, looking back, I still appreciate that my energy and drive were positive aspects of my leadership. I have also learned that my ravenous quest for tomorrow's victories often trumped my appreciation of each day. Yes, it is true that a sharp focus on the future is necessary. But enjoying the present and embracing your journey is also essential.

How many times in your life have you heard someone say, *Where did all those years go?* The reality is that hours, days, years, decades, and our lifetime slip by far too rapidly. We must make the journey count.

Just recently, I found myself speaking about how time is slipping away. Maybe I have just joined the ranks of those older folks, but I am starting to understand the wisdom in appreciating the journey itself.

Few of us stop and enjoy every day as we should. We are so busy with the distractions of day-to-day living that we become oblivious to our surroundings, our culture, and our magnificent interactions with the other humans. How many times have you said or thought, *I would give anything to have one more chance to go back and reset the clock so I could do [some task or relationship] better this time.*

Life has no time machine or reset button. Each day is a chance to start from wherever you are now. Living in the past can haunt us and make us hesitant to take action in the future.

The hustle and bustle of life—hurrying to get ready, rushing from place to place, always on a time schedule, worrying about insignificant things—prevents us from enjoying the essence of life. Enjoying the essence is illustrated for me in how I enjoy my children, versus how I relish my grandchildren. While raising our children, we were so worried about all the details, such as schools, homework, time management, clean rooms and everything in between, that we often failed to enjoy our children. With grandchildren, we usually don't muck up our relationship with all those details. We just enjoy them and love them without the pressure. In other words, we enjoy the essence of life with them. I have often said, "If I had known how great it was to have grandchildren, I would have had them first."

I look back on my life, and I wish I had taken the time to stop and realize how great every day really was. Living by my own advice, I realize that I cannot have a do-over. The best I can hope for is to communicate my sentiments and experiences to other people so they may benefit from my hard-learned advice.

This fact was driven home for me recently. I was teaching in Myrtle Beach, South Carolina. The class began, as usual, on a Monday morning. During the morning introductions, I was quizzing the students about their mindset and how they approach every day.

"How many of you got up this morning, and the first thing out of your mouth or on your mind was something negative? How many of you started your day by expressing your displeasure at having to wake up so early?"

One of the students in the back of the room replied, "You mean, how many of us said, *Damn!*, when we got up this morning?"

The entire class laughed, and we went on to discuss how important it is to embrace each day and not wake up with a *Damn, I dread today* attitude, but with a positive tone.

I got to know this student better as the week progressed. His name was Paul Frick. He was a deputy supervisor with the Warren County Sheriff's Department in Missouri. Paul was also a part-time police chief in a small town in the same county. I thought this was odd to be a full-time deputy and a part-time chief. I also thought that it was no wonder he started his day with a *Damn!*, because he had two tough jobs, and I'm sure he was often exhausted.

Paul explained that the small town where he served as part-time chief had a small budget and a small force of officers. He went on to say that because it was a peaceful place, they did not usually need police service on a full-time basis. So Paul worked as a chief a few hours a week to provide leadership and to fill in the gaps.

Paul and I had several small but meaningful conversations throughout the rest of the week.

On Friday, when the class was over, Paul Frick came up to me to say goodbye. We talked for a few minutes, and I will never forget what he told me.

"Chief, I have learned a lot this week, and I thank you for that. But what is more important is that I learned a lot about myself. You know, on Monday, when you asked that question to the class about our first thoughts in the morning, about whether we started our day with *Damn?* Well, I have thought about that a lot. I have decided I am not going to have any more damn-type mornings. I am going to enjoy life to the fullest and really try to embrace each day."

I congratulated Paul on his new way of looking at each day, and encouraged him to keep in touch with me.

I had also made quick friends with a couple other Warren County deputies in the class, and in August, I received an e-mail from one of those deputies. His e-mail read: "I regret to inform you that yesterday, Deputy Paul Frick was killed in an on-duty automobile accident in Warren County."

I had to sit down and gather myself for a moment. I couldn't help but flashback to what Paul had told me as he left the classroom in April. His words had more meaning than I had understood at the time. I sure hope that Paul enjoyed every day until his last, and that he did not burden himself with too many damn-type mornings.

I have had the honor and privilege to meet five presidents of the United States, and to have visited the White House on five separate occasions. I attended the FBI Academy, the Secret Service School, and I even spent a week in Israel as a guest of the Israeli Foreign Ministry. These are all great things, but I never took the time to stop and say, *Wow!* Sometimes we don't recognize the most significant things in our life are happening to us until they've passed us by.

Take the time to prepare for the future, but please remember that each day is a special gift. Vow to relish each morning and enjoy the journey.

I have used these simple but effective methods to help me enjoy the moment and embrace life's journey.

Tips for Enjoying Each Day

- Slow down. Don't be in such a hurry to get to everywhere you're going. I am often in such a hurry to get somewhere that when I get there, I'm not sure how I got there.

- Adjust your mindset to look at the world from a positive perspective.

- Don't let other people's emergencies create chaos in your life. I have found that the more I react to other people's problems, the more chaotic my life is. Don't get sucked into their drama.

- Realize that you are only on this earth for a certain amount time. Enjoy it. There are so many amazing things you are missing by being in a hurry.

- Enjoy where you live. Visit places in your area that you have not been to before. Find joy and peace in your backyard.

CHAPTER 12

BE A GOOD LISTENER

Good listeners have a huge advantage.
For one, when they engage in conversation,
they make people "feel" heard.
They "feel" that someone really understands
their wants, needs, and desires.
And for good reason;
a good listener does care to understand.

—Simon Sinek

At what age were you taught to speak? Most of us were taught in the first year of life, or shortly thereafter. Certainly, by the age of two we were speaking our minds and demanding things we wanted.

At what age were we taught to listen? Interestingly, for most of us the answer is never. We were never taught *how* to listen. We learned to listen by hearing others talk, and by assimilating the messages.

Listening is a vital life skill, yet we receive no training on how to do it well. The importance of good listening cannot be understated. Over the years, I have come across many people who are great listeners, and many others who are not.

I separate listening into five categories:

1. *Ignoring listening* occurs when the person you are speaking with ignores what you are saying. They may appear to hear you, but they are not absorbing the words you are speaking. Who does this? A rebellious child, an uninterested spouse, or an upset friend may all be excellent at ignoring what you are saying.

2. *Selective listening* is when someone only listens to portions of what is being said. Politicians use this type of listening a great deal. You know what I'm talking about. When you shake a politician's hand, they are often looking around the room to see who else is there. Sometimes they are already looking at the next person near you, even though you may still be speaking to them.

I know of one politician who has mastered the ability to listen selectively while making you believe that you are getting his full attention. Bill Clinton is a master at the art of making you feel he is fully engaged in your conversation. I remember going to the White House with a lieutenant from our agency in the mid-1990s while Clinton was president. We were invited to a White House South Lawn ceremony followed by a short meet and greet with President Clinton. We had heard how charismatic and engaging this president was when you met him.

Shortly after the ceremony, President Bill Clinton came to the receiving line and met the guests who were there. This was the first time I had met him face-to-face, although I had worked his security detail as a local counterpart to the Secret Service agents. All the rumors were true. In that brief encounter, I was amazed at President Bill Clinton's ability to make me feel like I was the only person in the room he was interested in speaking with. Even if Clinton's listening was a little selective, it did not show. That president gave me the strong impression that he listened to me with his full attention.

3. *Techno listening* is superficial listening while you are texting, checking e-mails, or browsing your electronic devices. Unfortunately, it is fast becoming the new way of listening. It amounts to mildly ignoring others while multitasking. Anyone who has recently had a conversation with teenagers can definitely relate to this. But unfortunately, it is not limited to our youth. Techno listening has reached epidemic proportions for all age groups. Many of us in the older generations are doing the same thing. This is not only a failure to listen, but a failure to communicate with respect. If you question my assertion of this new wave of listening, take a few moments to observe others in conversation.

4. *Attentive listening* is true listening. It means not interrupting and not forming your responses before the person stops speaking. Listening attentively requires that you stop, look, and listen to the speaker. This is almost a lost art form. Looking someone in the eye when they speak, and actively listening, makes for golden communication.

When my twin boys were young, I remember teaching them how to correctly greet people and shake their hands. I told them to make eye contact, smile, and shake the person's hand, all the while listening to what the person had to say and remembering their names. It is amazing how much of a first impression you can make by just simply listening attentively to others.

5. *Listening to understand* is listening with the intent to recognize the needs of the other person, and to thoroughly understand their viewpoint. This means not adding our own biases, opinions, or stories. We often listen with the intent to reply and to express our own opinion. This is a hard habit to break. Next time you listen to someone, see how quick you are to interject your personal experiences

and viewpoint, rather than to listen to what the other person has to say. In fact, while the other person is speaking, we often block them out so that we can formulate our response. We are so accustomed to replying that it is an automatic reflection to speak instead of listen.

Being a good listener is key to hearing what is being said. I am reminded of a story I heard about Red Auerbach, the famous head coach of the Boston Celtics during their run of thirteen NBA Championships. Timeouts last for either twenty seconds or one minute, and Coach Auerbach had to communicate in a concise manner. He is quoted as saying, "It is not what you say that matters, but what people hear that matters."

Tips for Being a Good Listener

- Seek to understand the other person's viewpoint.
- Be Fully present.
- Avoid looking at your mobile devices.
- Look the person in the eye.
- Show empathy.
- Be careful with your body language.

CHAPTER 13

DON'T LET ANGER CONTROL YOU

So many people get involved with carrying grudges and having these moral battles with people, where they cast themselves as the righteous and the other guy is the dirt bag. They waste tons of energy on it, create all kinds of darkness around themselves and the other person. It gets you nothing.

—Stephen J. Cannell

Anger is part of everyday life. But the uncontrolled expression of anger often causes many problems. People sometimes allow anger to hijack their emotions, thus allowing rage to be the foundation of their decision-making. This can lead to dire consequences. Letting anger control you is like drinking the poison and wanting the other person to die.

In *Introduction to Buddhism*, Venerable Geshe Kelsang Gyatso says, "Anger is a response to feelings of unhappiness, which in turn arise whenever we meet with unpleasant circumstances."

Anger is an emotion that, when out of control, is used as an excuse to treat others badly. If you stay angry with them, you convince yourself you have a free rein to justify any negative behavior towards them. This can lead to inappropriate actions such as lying, threatening physical violence, or even exacting revenge.

Unfortunately, like many people, I have let anger get the best of me and cloud my judgment. This has not served me well as a leader. I remember facing a difficult decision regarding discipline of an employee. The employee was guilty of the infraction, but I enraged about what they had done. Fortunately, it did not lead to the dismissal of the employee, but the discipline was impacted by my anger.

Have you ever done or said something in a fit of anger, then justified it by thinking or saying, *I was ticked off, and they got what they deserved?* Uncontrolled anger arouses our most primitive feelings and causes us to strike back before we think. Unfortunately, the ones who are closest to us often receive the brunt of our angry outbursts.

If left unresolved, uncontrolled anger can also lead to the formation of grudges. Grudges are deeper-seated forms of anger. Cambridge Dictionary describes *grudge* as "a strong feeling of anger and dislike for a person who treated you badly."

The challenge of controlling your anger and living a grudge-free life can be daunting. Each day, we are faced with difficult situations that may anger us, and sometimes we revert to an emotional reaction rather than a smart one. We take the actions of others personally. We allow their actions to control us. We allow circumstances to dictate how we react and how we respond. In essence, our anger can control our lives.

What makes me most upset is when I think someone is doing something to personally offend me or cause me harm. In other words, when I begin to perceive someone's motives as harmful, this enhances my anger. Once I get in that negative frame of mind, it becomes harder and harder to stay in control. Anger breeds more anger, so we need to control the emotional impulses that anger can cause.

I have adopted an approach to help me control myself and to think before I act. I am not perfect in my ability to control my anger, but this has helped me. Imagine you are faced with a situation that upsets you. When are we faced with these scenarios, our reaction to them influences the outcome. So I have learned that how I respond is key. You have two ways you can deal with the situation: You can either respond to the situation, or react. If you respond, you are more deliberate and patient. If you react, you are more emotional, and can inflame the situation. I have often reacted when I should have responded, thereby making the situation worse.

I have created formulas out of my own experiences, and by examining what happens when I let anger control me. Anger usually begins when people take the actions of others personally. Then the person weighs the actions and judges the other person's motives. This is often followed by flavoring our judgment of others' actions as either malicious or not (usually malicious, by our own nature). Then we react with negative actions, which will end with a negative outcome. While sometimes these are only short-term consequences, they are most often long-term because we want to hang on to those negative feelings caused by negative interactions. We can avoid this by not taking the actions of others personally, or by giving them the benefit of the doubt when it does feel personal.

The formulae below describe both:

$$\text{Personal (P)} + \text{Motive (M)} + \text{Malice (M)}$$
$$= \text{Negative Response (NR)}$$
$$= \text{Negative Outcome (NO)}$$

$$\text{Not Personal (NP)} + \text{Benefit of Doubt (BD)}$$
$$= \text{Positive Response (PR)}$$
$$= \text{Positive Outcome (PO)}$$

To control my anger, I have learned to give the person who has offended me the benefit of the doubt. I try to keep an open mind and not be so quick to judge their motives. I try to see things from their point of view instead of presuming they have a malicious intent. The second I allow malice to enter into my thought process, the harder it is to control my thoughts and emotions. Thinking and acting from pure, unbridled emotion usually ends badly for everyone. It ends up with an emotional hijacking that leads to nonproductive outcomes.

The key to the formula is to adjust our attitude at the beginning of the interaction to avoid overreaction or aggression. But if we do find ourselves responding as if the infraction was personal, we can adjust our response by giving others the benefit of the doubt. This will lessen the motive and malice portion, to a manageable degree that you have time to think.

Controlling anger is a key to self-control, which is an ultimate key to being an effective leader.

Tips for Controlling Your Anger

- Think before you speak.
- Take a breath.
- Practice empathy.
- Give the person the benefit of the doubt.
- Don't be judgmental

CHAPTER 14

LEADERS ARE READERS

Not all readers are leaders, but all leaders are readers.

—Harry S. Truman

There was a time when I hated to read. It was during what I call the dark period of my life, when I had minimal discipline or direction. I had no idea where I was going. This was right after high school, shortly after I played professional baseball in the minor league, for the Minnesota Twins, and just before I became a police officer.

During my high school years, I focused on sports, not academics. I was a terrible student. This certainly was no secret to my teachers. All through high school, I was a sports junkie, a jock. I especially loved playing baseball. Being a good baseball player gave me the opportunity to sign a professional contract right out of high school. Unfortunately, I spent most of my time playing sports and participating in other extracurricular activities. I was certainly not studying or working on school assignments any more than I absolutely had to. As a result, I did not develop good reading or writing skills. I was barely functional when it came to both, and I struggled with the simplest of reading assignments. As a result, I did not enjoy reading.

After my minor league career ended, I became a police officer with the Asheville Police Department, and quickly realized that I needed to not only improve my reading and writing skills, but I needed to further my education. So I enrolled at Asheville

Community College and began a course of study in criminal justice. The college required students to take entrance exams to evaluate where they stood on reading, writing, and arithmetic. I took the perfunctory tests, and because of my inability to read or write well, the scores were abysmally low. I scored in the bottom 20 percent of the students who were accepted into the college, and therefore had to negotiate my way into school. I agreed to go to the learning lab to improve my skills. I would spend at least one hour in the learning lab for every day I attended class.

I was not surprised at my scores on the entrance examination, considering the minuscule amount of time I had devoted to my studies. Still, I did not like how this made me feel.

There were several reasons for my poor academic performance. I had not been successful in my elementary attempts at reading and writing, and that ultimately led me to feel discouraged about ever improving. Like many people who experience failures, I did not want to admit it or continue to experience not being good at something, so I just didn't work on it. Because I was not poor at reading, I shied away from doing it, and the results were predictable. Like anything in life, the more success you have, the more you enjoy it, the more you work at it, and the easier it becomes. This was true for me with sports.

But while attending college, I realized I also needed to put in some extra training to become a better student, which, in turn, would benefit me professionally. Police officers need to write accurate and detailed reports that can withstand the scrutiny of the courts.

After a few short months of going to the learning lab, my skills began to improve dramatically. Remarkably, I found that I enjoyed reading and writing once I could do them well. It was in the learning lab that I developed a love for reading. I realized how reading can change you for the better and vastly improve the quality of your life.

Reading can open the world of knowledge for you. It provides a way to travel the world and explore things you can only dream of. Reading is the great equalizer. People rich and poor, short and tall, and from every corner of the globe and every station of life can learn and grow through reading. The works of the great scientists, renowned historians, wise philosophers, and capable leaders are all in books and articles, just waiting to be passed on to those who read them.

Dr. Thomas Barton, the first president of Greenville Technical College, is a visionary leader, and he enjoyed a tenure that lasted over thirty-five years. When Barton opened the doors in the early 1960s, Greenville Technical College was housed in a few small trailers on a donated parcel of land. By the end of his tenure, the college had enrolled over thirteen thousand students. The college had four satellite campuses and was known as a national leader in community college education.

Tom Barton is a personal friend of mine, and I worked with him on many law enforcement initiatives. During one of our conversations, we were talking about his ability to innovate. I noted how Barton brought fresh ideas to the campus on a weekly basis. I asked him what his secret was.

He replied, "I read a great deal."

I was a surprised by his simple response, but Tom said, "Every day, I make it a point to read articles, books, or journals about personal leadership. I read about other colleges and universities around the country, and what makes them successful. Very few people will invent a new wheel, but everyone can learn from how the first one was invented."

Although it had been years since I'd graduated, I once again learned a great deal about leadership from this enlightened college president.

Reading daily for personal instruction and professional development will set you apart from most leaders. Leaders think that on-the-job training is enough, and believe that most of their skills can be learned by trial and error alone. While I will never shortchange the value of the school of hard knocks, I know that we will learn more abundantly, deeper, and faster if our experience is supplemented by books and articles.

In short, reading allows you to benefit through a collection of research, knowledge, and experience—more than any one person could accrue in a lifetime!

In some leadership classes I teach, we have a small block of time each morning which we call Leaders are Readers. These classes are usually filled with senior management personnel. Most have master's or bachelor's degrees, and they are responsible for the safety of entire communities, and for the legal and social well-being of anywhere from dozens to thousands of employees. As part of the Leaders are Readers activity, each student shares a book or article they have read recently. The only criteria is that the reading material must be connected to the topic of leadership, and the material must have made an impact upon the student's life or career.

I am repeatedly amazed at the number of students who confess to not reading at all, or minimally. To those who are reluctant to read, I often say, "If I could give you a secret four-letter word that could change your life for the better and dramatically improve the quality of your life, would you want to hear it?"

In all cases, the person says yes.

I reply, "The secret word is...R-E-A-D."

In today's world, effective leaders must read. They must stay abreast of current trends by devoting time each day to reading. Technology, law, and social science are evolving at an unprecedented pace. One goal in my classes, just like in this book, is to remind leaders that reading relevant books and articles has become a necessary component to stay current in our craft.

Many people have a change of heart and a new appreciation for fresh information after they participate in my leadership classes. Perhaps when people consider this perspective, they will pick up a book. Since you have picked up this one, you are well on your way!

Tips to Create a Habit of Reading

- Select books that at your current reading comprehension level. If you have only read a few books or articles, don't choose material that is highly academic or requires a dictionary to understand what the author is saying. Stick to what connects to you.

- Read in short bursts, and take frequent breaks.

- Read about topics that you are interested in.

- Don't read every book chapter by chapter. Skip around to keep it interesting.

- Talk to others about what you are reading. You will be surprised how this begins some interesting conversations.

CHAPTER 15

LIFE'S REARVIEW MIRROR

Don't dwell on what went wrong.
Instead, focus on what to do next.
Spend your energies on moving forward
toward finding the answer.

—Denis Waitley

Living forward is not easy. Every day, we are constantly reminded of the past. A good friend of mine, Billy Presley (who unfortunately died at the age of forty-two, in a race car accident), once preached a sermon entitled, "You Can't Live Forward by Looking in Life's Rearview Mirror." There is a great deal of wisdom in that title, and like most of you, I try to live my life looking forward, with optimism and enthusiasm.

Unfortunately, we all live in the past. Daily, we are reminded of past pursuits and decisions, events and mistakes. This history is what we use to guide us into the new day. In short, we let yesterday's problems determine today's direction.

In line with Billy's sermon, imagine driving your car down a busy highway and paying no attention to what is occurring in front of you. Instead, you are constantly looking in the rearview mirror. The likelihood that you will have an accident is nearly guaranteed. Why? Because you are focusing your attention upon what is behind you, and not what is in front of you. I know this sounds simplistic, but it's true. We simply cannot drive forward—

at least, not well—if we are focused on the rearview mirror. Yes, we should use that rearview mirror to check on what is behind us, and even to remind us that things from the past us can creep up and cause a problem. But the main focus should be on what lies ahead of us—a new road, even if it contains a few curves.

How much better would your day be if you lived in the present or future and didn't worry about yesterday's problems? How many times have you experienced seemingly small problems at work, and then gone home thinking about them? Not only do you think about your difficulties, you may even obsess over them. That evening, while you relive and remain embroiled in the quandary, you miss the full experience of enjoying time with the family. Even when you go to work the next day, you can't focus on what needs to be done because you are so obsessed with yesterday's problems. This is not productive.

In our personal lives, we are even more likely to live in the past because our feelings are even more involved. Can you remember a time when someone close to you hurt your feelings or said something you didn't like? Did you spend days, or even years, not speaking to that person? Relationships are constantly affected by yesterday's dilemmas and the inability to live forward. As humans, we tend to let yesterday's feelings negatively affect today's opinions.

In my own life, I have witnessed family members who are so focused on what happened yesterday that they have a difficult time moving forward. They are trapped to the point of deadlock. Little progress or joy exists for them because they are still stuck on their past predicaments. I am not advocating that we erase what happened yesterday. It is not possible to do that. And I recognize and understand how important history is. But focusing too much on the past can seriously detract from the importance of tomorrow. Living forward requires a short memory and a special commitment to future endeavors.

Imagine that life is on a linear plane. How much do we live in each state—the past, the present, and the future? I would guess that most of us spend a lot of time dwelling upon the past, spending some time in the present, and then investing only a little creative energy into what lies ahead in the future. In *The 7 Mindsets to Live Your Ultimate Life*, Scott Shickler and Jeff Waller refer to research that says each of us have sixty-five thousand thoughts every day, but 95 percent of those thoughts are the same ones we had from yesterday. This would indicate that we spend much of our time in the past. At what cost to the road ahead?

The future is, literally, what we make it. By thinking and living forward, enthusiastically, we open up that glorious opportunity to notice every new opportunity we come across. Devoid of the burden of past psychological baggage, we can seize every chance to develop our thoughts, our creativity, and our passions to their fullest capability.

Living forward gives you tremendous potential and amazing power. It is a hallmark, an aptitude, and a mindset worthy of a great leader. Living forward requires focusing on the future and developing a plan for your life. We have a choice to go through life as a spectator reacting to our circumstances, or as an active participant taking control of our actions to determine our future. To live forward, you must let go of the past and see your challenges as opportunities to redirect your life.

Tips for Living Forward

- Let the past guide you, not control you.
- Enjoy the daily form of life. Recognize that the past is yesterday, the present is today, and the future is tomorrow.
- Slow down. Stop being in such a hurry.
- Understand that what you do today will have a major impact on tomorrow's results.
- Sweat the small stuff.

CHAPTER 16

BE DETERMINED

Failure will never overtake me
if my determination to succeed is strong enough.

—Og Mandino

I am always amazed when I watch a determined person at work. It is inspiring to see them grind through all types of obstacles while staying focused on getting the task accomplished. I would guess that all of us have met a person like this. Maybe we have even been like this ourselves. When you are determined, you don't let much, if anything, get in your way. This type of determination is required to be a good leader, but can be difficult to sustain.

Let's face it, during our lifetime, we are going to hear the word *no* hundreds of times—probably much more than we'll hear yes—and face many roadblocks. Remember a time when you wanted to do something important in your life. I would venture to say that before you got to the word yes, someone told you no multiple times. The test of determination is whether or not you move past that barricade.

I can remember a personal story that describes what having determination can do. When my father was ill and in the intensive care unit, he was scheduled for a heart procedure in the early morning hours. I was told by Dad's physician that I could visit him briefly in his room just before he was to be wheeled into the operating room. The doctor had already emphasized, more than once, that the procedure was risky and could result in my father's death. Without exactly saying so, the doctor was giving me a chance to say goodbye to my father just in case the worse happened.

If you have ever been in the ICU, you know that visiting hours are not the same as the rest of the hospital. Patient access is limited, usually by large doors and unrelenting hospital staff. These limitations are with good reason because patients in the ICU need peace and quiet, and the medical staff needs constant access to patients for treatment and monitoring. Doctors and nurses must be able to hear a wide variety of medical equipment which may signal changes in a patient's condition. Therefore, ICU visiting hours are usually scheduled incrementally, and only for a short time.

As I arrived outside the intensive care unit, I phoned the nurse's station to be allowed in. The nurse who answered the phone informed me that my father was leaving shortly for the operating room. She advised that I would be able to get a glimpse of him as he passed by the waiting area on the way to surgery, but there was no time for a visit.

I informed the nurse that the doctor had already given me permission, but she told me they were busy and could not accommodate my request. I would simply have to wait. I pleaded my case again, and again I was denied by the superficially polite, but unshakable nurse. Everything in her words and tone sent the signal that she had other patients to attend to, and that I was becoming a bother. The nurse directed me to sit quietly in the waiting room, where I would have the opportunity to see my father pass by on a gurney.

When I hung up the phone with the imperialistic nurse, I was furious. And instead of settling for her edict, I contacted my father's physician. The doctor assured me he could help.

Within five minutes, I was allowed back to see my father. To this day, I do not know what the doctor did, or who he spoke to, but I will be forever grateful for that his compassion and intervention. The moments my father and I spent before his surgery were priceless. I did not want my dad to face the fears of this dangerous surgery alone, especially in his critical medical condition. To be honest, it was a critical time for me, too, as I did not want to miss the opportunity to share this precious, perhaps final, time with my dad.

Thanks to God and good medicine, Dad recovered. Still, I will never forget those cherished moments we spent together. Each minute we spent in that sterilized ICU took on a special meaning, as we both knew that time might be our last together. Even now, our relationship is stronger than ever, largely because we reached an understanding of just how precious life is, and how much we mean to each other. My determination to see my father resulted in treasured memories that would never have happened had I taken no for an answer.

I have often told my sons that if their *yes* is more determined than other people's *no*, they can rest assured that they will accomplish their goals. Fortunately, I have come out ahead in most police chief promotional processes simply because of my determination and unwillingness to fail.

Determination is a powerful force, especially when it is fueled by courage. I have never heard a story as compelling as the one I heard from a student one morning. I was teaching a class in Knoxville, Tennessee. As I often do, I asked the students to read an article or book on leadership that night, then make a short oral presentation the next day. The students were free to choose any medium they wished, so long as they let me and the class know why it was important to them.

A female officer in attendance sat near the front and had not been talkative the first day. I figured she was just more of the quiet type. On the second day of training, right before we began class, the officer asked me whether her report had to be from a book, or if it could be from another source.

Always open to good ideas, but cautious about students who try to duck work, I asked her, "Well, no, not exactly. What do you have in mind?"

The officer said that she had a brother who'd influenced her, and that she would like to share his story. I was intrigued, so I agreed and asked her if she would like to go first.

The officer replied, "No, I can wait."

As the morning reports progressed, it became obvious that all were inspiring accounts of leadership. I noticed that the officer was increasingly fidgety. To relieve her growing anxiety, I asked her if she would like to go next. I also mentioned that we had a break coming up, so we would take that break right after her presentation. She agreed.

The officer stood and began telling her story. She continued to show signs of nervousness, and even seemed shy as she started talking about her younger brother, Randy. She recounted how, even as a young fellow, "Randy was so active and had such a bright smile." She added that Randy was her favorite sibling because of the joy he brought to the family.

The officer spoke of how she and her brothers and sisters had lived in government-subsidized housing for most of their lives. As a huge smile spread across her face, she described how Randy, even as a little fellow, always loved pro wrestling. Apparently, Randy thought he was hot stuff. He often ran around the house, grabbed his other brothers and sisters, and pretended to be one of the famous wrestlers of the day.

One day, when Randy was eleven years old, the play became too rough. One of the other brothers grabbed Randy and put him in a famous wrestling move called a suplex. This move is where one person picks the other up by his waist, then over his head, and falls backward. The officer made it clear that all the kids in the family knew the suplex move and had done it hundreds of times. Usually, Randy would jump up growling, shouting, and laughing, then counter his brother's tactic. But this time, the fall was bad. Randy lay there motionless, crying out in pain. As the family rushed to his aid, it became obvious that Randy had injured his spine, and had maybe even broken his neck. The wrestling move had caused instant paralysis of his lower body.

The family rushed Randy to the hospital. The officer recounted, "He looked so helpless and so young." As she told the story, she began to cry a little. She described the look on Randy's face and how he looked so pitiful.

The officer remembered how little Randy had looked at her, smiled, and told her, matter-of-factly, "Sis, this was nobody's fault, and so no one is to blame. God obviously has a plan for me not to walk like regular people. So we have to trust his plan. Besides, you must always remember that I will never give up. One day, I will walk again."

The officer went on to tell us how difficult this hospital visit was for her. She described how seeing little Randy lying there brought so much pain. She took us all through the emotions of desperately wanting to change what had happened, but knowing she could not. She also shared that somehow it gave her comfort to hear such courage and determination from someone as young as Randy. More than ever before, she was proud of her little brother.

The officer described the next few years as gut-wrenching. It was tough to see her brother struggle so hard against all odds. Everyone in the family was devastated by this accident, and it changed the lives of the entire family.

"Randy's spirit was injured but not broken," she told us.

After his injuries stabilized, Randy began an exercise regimen that would be difficult even for people who can walk. He even began to race competitively in his wheelchair. Randy was a source of strength and inspiration for the family. As he turned twenty, his desire to walk never faded. He worked relentlessly to try to regain that ability. By then, his big sister had become a police officer.

Then one evening, while the officer was at work, she received a call that Randy had been involved in a traffic accident, and had been transported to the hospital emergency room. Not knowing what to expect, she rushed to the hospital. As the young officer arrived, she was met by a family member who shared the bad news. The officer learned that Randy had been rolling his wheelchair down a sidewalk, training for an upcoming race, when a drunk driver swerved off the road and hit him.

The officer told our class, "I couldn't believe this was happening to my brother after all he had already been through."

She entered the hospital room where the doctors were treating her brother, and found him surrounded by several doctors and nurses. He was covered in blood, and tubes were running out of every limb.

Randy realized his sister had arrived, and motioned for her to come closer. As she leaned down, Randy just looked up at her and smiled like he always did. In a weakened voice, he whispered, "Don't worry, sis. I am not going to give up. This is just a minor setback. I told you that one day I will walk again."

The officer had only a few minutes with her brother because the medical staff was rushing him to surgery. She recalled the agonizing time spent in the waiting room, hoping for the best. But Randy never made it out of surgery. He died shortly after he was taken to the operation room. Her little brother, her hero, would never get that opportunity to walk again.

As the officer began to take her seat in the classroom, she said, "Somehow I know that where Randy is now, he is getting that chance. He is not only walking again, but he is running with the wind."

As you can imagine, silence had fallen over the entire classroom by then. As I looked around this group of tough and experienced police officers, there was not a dry eye in the room. But one thing was certain: all of us had witnessed true determination.

Randy's story is one of grit and determination. As leaders, those qualities are imperative to success. Being determined is not just hanging in there. It is the essence of increasing your chances of being successful. Randy's determination is an example to all.

In *Last Lecture*, the author, Randy Pausch, a professor at Carnegie Melon University, is diagnosed with terminal pancreatic cancer and given less than six months to live. He was asked, if he had a chance to write his last lecture, what would it be. Pausch chose to write on about determination and how it impacts your life. He gives a great example of determination in his analogy of a brick wall. He says that brick walls are placed before us not to stop us, but to reveal our level of determination. He goes on to say that determination helps us find a way around, over, under, or through those walls.

How many brick walls have you faced? Like many of us, I bet you are facing one now. How resolved are you to get past it? Your level of determination has a direct correlation to your level of success.

Tips for Being Determined

- Stay focused on getting through the challenge.
- Control your fear of failure.
- Remain positive.
- Be aware of your self-talk.
- Surround yourself with people who believe in you.
- Don't let a momentary setback stop you.

II

LEADING
OTHERS

This section encompasses what I have learned about leading others. Being a leader means that you achieve goals through the efforts of others, which is dependent upon their ability to work well with each other.

As we become a more interrelated and interdependent society, teamwork has never been more important than it is today. Leaders must motivate, inspire, and provide a vision for others to follow. I believe that the key role of any leader is to grow others, and to do so you must first be able to lead them.

In the following chapters, I will provide you with leadership lessons that have helped mold me into the leader I am today. My goal is that these lessons enhance your leadership competencies while encouraging you to develop others. No leader can exist without followers. This means that leaders must be aware of their impact on those they lead.

As a leader, you are ultimately responsible for the leadership behaviors of your subordinates. Obviously, it is impossible to control the actions of others. But you can influence their views on leadership behavior.

Most of us grew up with the Golden Rule: treat others as you want to be treated. It is imperative for all leaders to abide by this. It should also be noted that leading others is a privilege, not a right. Leadership is not a transactional interaction between a leader and subordinates. A key motivator for others is helping them to grow not only as a subordinate, but as a person, which requires qualitative interactions to help them move forward.

CHAPTER 17

BE PASSIONATE

There is no passion to be found playing small—
in settling for a life that is less than
the one you are capable of living.

—Nelson Mandela

Passion is what drives you and gives you purpose—an intrinsic motivation that propels you forward. It is a strong feeling or desire based on a commitment that makes you get up in the morning and welcome the day ahead. No matter how bad the day before was, or how bad the day you are facing is, you continue to move forward and embrace the challenges. Passion is about heart, or *heart-set*. The best leaders are passionate, and this passion will help you connect with the people you lead.

John Maxwell, in his book *21 Irrefutable Laws of Leadership*, wrote, "You can't move people to action unless you first move them with emotion. The heart comes before the head."

True passion will naturally draw out feelings and connections with others.

How many people do you know who are passionate about their job? I would guess, not many! That is an unfortunate fact of life. Most people are not doing what they are passionate about. They are trapped in the doldrums of life, working to live instead of living to work. Many people spend their lives stuck in a job out of necessity, instead of doing what they love to do.

I'm one of the lucky ones because I made a career choice I was passionate about. When I first started working as a police officer, I was absolutely passionate about being a cop. I was even surprised that I got paid for doing what I loved.

To give you an example of how much I loved my job, I remember standing at the front desk of the police department, receiving my biweekly check, and looking at my pay stub. I had cleared $180 for two weeks of work. While this was in 1980, it still was not much, even by the standards of that time. I noticed my lieutenant, Ralph Cook, standing next to me, opening his check. Lieutenant Cook was so close to me that I couldn't help but see that he had made $350 for that same two weeks! Although the lieutenant had made almost twice as much, it was clear to me that the pay didn't matter. I would have been a cop for free. Yes, I loved it that much. My heart and soul belonged to police work.

All my life, my mom had told me, "Son, if you love your job, you won't work a day in your life. But if you hate it, you'll work every day."

These are wise words, and while looking at the pay stub in 1980, I realized I was experiencing that. What an honor and a privilege to find my life's passion at the early age of twenty!

In his book *Highest Duty*, Captain Sullenberger describes how he found his life's passion at the ripe age of five. Sully knew he wanted to be a pilot. Thank God he was in control of US Airways Flight 1549, on January 15, 2009. Sullenberger's skills and experience, coupled with his passion for flying, help save all 155 passengers on board when he landed his plane into the Hudson River. I can only imagine that the people on board were especially glad that Captain Sullenberger was the guy at the controls that day. Imagine if the pilot had been someone who was only half-engaged with his job? The outcome may have been totally different.

In my thirty-plus years in law enforcement, there was never a day that I got up and dreaded going to work. Now that doesn't mean I didn't face some tough days. Heck, I faced many days when I wondered if I would survive another one. But I did, and I credit my passion for getting me through those tough times.

Ask yourself: Am I passionate about what I do? Would I do this if I didn't have to? What would I really like to be doing?

I know it is difficult, if not impossible, to just quit your job, and I am certainly not telling you to do that. But are you passionate about what you do? If not, then it may be time to re-evaluate. How do you do that?

It is important to understand that finding your life's passion is paramount to discovering what it is that you should be doing. I have had many discussions with my sons over the past years, about discovering their passion.

Many people are either successful in their a career, are making a fair wage, or have great benefits and feel certain they cannot just up and quit. Their mind keeps telling them that leaving the job does not make sense. Yet they are miserable and feel trapped. What are they to do?

The transition to begin moving toward incorporating your passion into everyday life will be a difficult. But what is the alternative? Live your life to the fullest. The only way to do that is to enjoy every day. Helping to create passion in others will greatly enhance your ability as a leader to get things done. A person with passion will always outperform a person without it. Passion is the stick that stirs the drink. It brings everything together.

Tips for Finding and Keeping Your Passion

- Be realistic. This means keeping your ability to incorporate your passion into your life real. You did not get into a rut overnight, nor will you get out of it overnight.

- Take inventory of your life. Find out exactly where you are and how you can take steps to change things.

- Begin with a *yes* attitude. When you are trying to improve your life, you will always be told you can't do it. Your *yes* has to be stronger and more determined than other's *no*.

- Begin to find ways to incorporate your passion into everyday life. Do it slowly. Start with steps that are easy to accomplish. On weekends or in your spare time, find ways to network with people who share your passion.

- Develop a mature approach regarding your passion. Your passion has the power and potential to alter your life in a positive way. Embrace it. Become serious about your passion.

CHAPTER 18

HAVE A CLEAR MISSION

A leader is a person who knows the way,
goes the way and shows the way.

—John Maxwell

Having a clear mission for your professional and personal life provides you with direction and focus for all of life's journeys. What would you say if I were to ask, *Do you live your life by default or by design?* If you are like most of us, you would probably say you live by default. Few of us live our lives by design. Instead, we tend to live the life that others want for us. All of us are influenced by the actions of others, but it is up to us to steer our lives in the direction that we, as individuals, want to go.

I know from experience that if you have children, you are living mostly by default. Their needs far outweigh ours (rightfully so), but still, this causes a default lifestyle. Even though they are our children, we need to keep in mind that maintaining control of our lives is key to having a sense of direction.

Living by default is unfulfilling and leads to boredom. Every day seems to be the same. We go to work and do our jobs, and then we return home and watch TV or search the Internet. We go to bed, wake up the next day, and repeat the same cycle. We live day after day as if the future was already predetermined.

We each have around sixty-five thousand thoughts per day, according to a study cited in *The 7 Mindsets To Live Your Ultimate*

Life by Scott Schickler and Jeff Waller. That sounds like a lot. But according to the research, 95 percent of those thoughts are the same thoughts that we had the day before. They also found that 80 percent of the sixty-five thousand thoughts were negative. This explains why some people are both trapped in the past and have a negative outlook on life.

Most of us intend to do our best and get the most out of life, but somehow it never happens. Developing a life's mission can help change this by providing more direction, and thus, more satisfaction as you attain your goals.

Most organizations have a mission statement. We seem to accept the notion that organizations have missions, but people do not. Nothing is further from the truth. People should have a personal mission. Even though we witness the benefits of mission-driven companies, we often fail to see the importance of developing a mission-driven life.

One of my favorite baseball personalities of all time is Yogi Berra. He stated it well when he said, "If you don't know where you are going, you will end up somewhere else."

Mission statement formation can be simple, but it requires some work. I will help you get started.

There is no right or wrong way to write a mission statement. A personal mission statement will yield clarity and purpose for your life. It helps define who you are and how you will live. Your mission statement is a guide—if it's meaningful to you, that's all that matters.

One important idea to keep in mind is that mission statements are meant to be dynamic, not static. Please understand that once you write your mission statement, you will need to revisit it at least once a year to update your focus. This process will give it new life and meaning while keeping you on the right track.

Now, let's get started.

Tips for Writing a Clear Mission Statement

- Brainstorm what is needed for you to be fulfilled. It may help to separate your ideas into categories. For example, you could consider the four parts of your well-being: mental, physical, social, and spiritual.

- Draft a paragraph of what is important to you and what you wish to accomplish.

- After completing the first draft, refine the words and pare it down.

- Think about the second draft for a day or so, and then refine it one more time. Now it should have structure and meaning.

- After completion, it should be reviewed at least twice a year to make sure it is relevant and in-sync with your life's pursuits and direction. As you grow personally, you will grow as a leader.

CHAPTER 19

KEEP PROMISES

Keep every promise you make and
only make promises you can keep.

—Anthony Hitt

Leaders should always do what they say they will do. This sounds trivial, but it is true. Even simple things like, *I'll call you tomorrow*, or *I'll get back in touch with you*, reflect on your character as a leader. Failing to do the simple things matters to people. You are only as good as your word.

People judge the small things as a sign of your character and credibility. Not keeping your word erodes your employees' trust. Although a small promise such as, *I will call you*, seems harmless, following through matters.

While teaching a leadership class in the Washington, DC area, I was talking about how important it is to keep your word. I asked the students to share any experiences they might remember regarding keeping this topic. I was surprised when one student began sharing from a book she had read years before. The book was *Horton Hatches the Egg* by Dr. Seuss. At first I thought it strange that a police officer would reference a children's book in an adult leadership class, especially in a room full of potentially sarcastic cops. But as the officer began to explain the book's contents, it became obvious that she had identified a premier example of keeping your word.

In the book, Horton is an elephant who is duped into sitting on an egg by a sly chicken. Horton promises to sit on the egg, no matter what. He keeps his word through all types of weather and adverse conditions, even at the threat of death. During each challenging circumstance, Horton always says, "I meant what I said, and I said what I meant. An elephant is faithful one hundred percent!" At the end of the book, Horton is so successful in keeping his word that the baby hatched from the egg resembles him, not the chicken.

As that young police officer noted, keeping your word has a profound effect on others.

During the 9/11 attacks on the World Trade Center, Mayor Rudy Giuliani led the response and recovery, which was undoubtedly among of the most trying times in the history of New York, and likely, our nation. In his book, *Leadership*, Giuliani talks about the importance of keeping your word and making sure you fulfill promises. He recommends that leaders "under promise and over deliver."

Promises are important. The inability to keep your word will invariably damage your trustworthiness with employees—and everyone else in your life.

Failure to keep promises can damage your credibility. It also damages the relationships you hold dear. I was a talented high school baseball player, and was proud of what I had accomplished. First, I made the high school team and earned a starting spot. Then I was voted onto the all-star team. I was even getting some interest from pro scouts.

Before each game, I would ask my dad to come and see me play. He was a sheriff's deputy in Asheville, and was leading a busy life, but I wanted to share my success with him and make him proud of me. My father would always say, "I will get off early today and be at the park to see you." So I would begin each game by searching the stands, just to see if Dad was there. Unfortunately, he usually could not get off work in time to watch me play. I only remembered him showing up to one or two games my entire senior year. I can remember how this affected me in a negative way. I became angry, and it took me years to move past my anger and forgive my dad.

From this, I learned that keeping promises is important, especially with relationships you hold dear. Our brain keeps a log of promises that are made to us, and whether they are kept. We create an emotional sticky note for those promises, and we remember when someone breaks them.

Can you remember how a leader's failure to keep promises affected you? You were probably disappointed and thought twice about trusting their word again. Leaders need to understand that promises are important, and the ability to be counted on, even with the small stuff, makes a difference. Your word is your bond—and your reputation!

Tips for Keeping Promises

- Understand that your word is your bond.
- See the promise from the other person's point of view.
- Remember that there are no small commitments. If you said you would do it, then it's important.
- Don't make promises you can't keep. Before you commit, evaluate whether or not you have the ability to follow through.
- Remember that the gratification you get from making the promise will be long gone when you don't keep it.
- If something does come up, and you won't be able to keep your promise, let the person know in advance and explain the reason.
- Great leaders seek to under-promise and over-deliver.

CHAPTER 20

BE COURAGEOUS

Courage is not about being afraid to do something.
It is about being afraid and doing it anyway.

—Anonymous

Courage is the ability to stand up for what is right, no matter what the circumstances or the consequences. And as leader, you will constantly face situations that challenge your ability to be courageous and do what is right.

Leaders must be courageous when facing the obstacles that get in the way of doing business. The ability to draw from your experiences, both positive and negative, can assist you in exhibiting courage. Your potential as a leader will never be realized unless you exhibit courage.

The human personality often reacts in a confrontational way. Leaders must fight this and respond with courage. They must understand and accept that every stance they take, every decision they make, has the potential to draw fire. And yet, even knowing the criticism they'll face, they are called to act within the scope of doing what is right for all, instead of what is right for the few.

Courage comes from within, and for some leaders, courage comes naturally. Other leaders have to develop it. Whatever your courage level may be, you must put in the effort to maintain it.

An example of exhibiting courage is evaluating and providing accurate and productive feedback to those you lead. This can become troublesome if you have worked with these individuals for years. Our instincts may tell us to go easy and not be too critical of employees we have a good relationship with. We tend to be general and unspecific in our constructive critiques, letting them slide. This is counterproductive to personal and organizational productivity.

Most of us live in three zones of comfort: the comfort zone, the uncomfortable zone, and the panic zone. Imagine three circles inside of a larger circle. The inner circle is our comfort zone, and contains our homes, family, or favorite chair. The second circle is the uncomfortable zone. We experience this when we go to a new place and are unsure of our surroundings. The panic zone is when we are scared. An example would be the feeling of being lost, or experiencing large upheavals such as the death of a loved one, moving to a new city, or starting a new job. When we are in this zone, we tend to react fearfully and let our emotions dominate our decision-making.

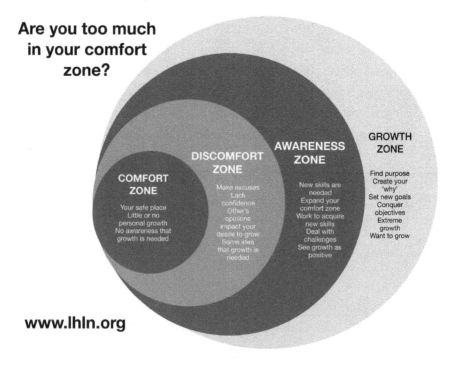

Are you too much in your comfort zone?

COMFORT ZONE
Your safe place
Little or no personal growth
No awareness that growth is needed

DISCOMFORT ZONE
Make excuses
Lack confidence
Other's opinions impact your desire to grow
Some idea that growth is needed

AWARENESS ZONE
New skills are needed
Expand your comfort zone
Work to acquire new skills
Deal with challenges
See growth as positive

GROWTH ZONE
Find purpose
Create your 'why'
Set new goals
Conquer objectives
Extreme growth
Want to grow

www.lhln.org

I have experienced this zone frequently in my personal and professional life. If I was not aware, giving into the feeling of panic would have prevented me from encountering new experiences that enriched my life.

Some people get complacent in their job, school, or personal life. They get too used to in their comfort zones. In this zone, most things are familiar, and change is almost nonexistent. If change does occur, it is usually at a snail's pace, and therefore non-threatening. Courage is the virtue that can lead you out of this comfort zone and into what I refer to as the challenge zone. The panic zone is a place of change, where you push yourself to the limits of your abilities. Courage enables us—in fact, forces us—to accept our failures and move beyond them. Even if we have immeasurable skills and abilities, we are likely to fail from time to time. Terrific! Periodic failure provides the springboard to move forward. Each failure makes us realize what areas we fall short in. It provides the opportunity for us to make changes and to succeed at a level greater than before.

The greater our courage, the more effective we will be as leaders. It does take courage to speak up and to express what we believe to guide us in the best course of action. We may have to defy old habits and ways of doing things whether those ingrained patterns of behavior belong to ourselves, to other people, or to an entire organization. Leaders have to reach deep inside their value systems and share their unique perspective with the people they lead. True leaders make a difference. They create improvements in people and in entire systems by taking what they know in their hearts to be the best course of action.

With policing, this can be seen most visibly in issues surrounding excessive force and corruption. When leaders give in to fear and pressure, these problems are exacerbated. But it doesn't have to be like this. Excessive force and corruption have been driven out of police organizations when brave leaders stand up and act courageously.

Expressing courage is not without cost—especially when it matters most. Being a courageous leader extracts a toll on you personally and professionally.

In "How to Cultivate the Courage to Deal with Daily Activities," originally published in the Gaiam Life newsletter, Polly Campbell states: "And while there is little empirical evidence that explains unequivocally how courage manifests, preliminary research and anecdotal evidence does suggest that people who act courageously share some common behaviors. Those commonalities offer clues into what we can all do to boost our own Courage Quotient."

Tips for Increasing Your Courage Quotient

- Prepare for potential outcomes. Long before firefighters run into a burning building, they practice and train for the experience. You can do the same. Look for ways to mitigate the potential for damage in the situations you face. Educate yourself. Know your facts. Preparing for a presentation? Practice the speech repeatedly. About to blow the whistle on workplace impropriety? Document the infractions. If you're ready to leave a bad marriage, find a safe place to go before you call it quits. Ready to follow your dream? Make a list of some of the things you'll do first to gain momentum.

- Step out of your comfort zone. Take baby steps into low-risk situations that make you uncomfortable. That will help boost your confidence and courage when it comes to coping with more difficult scenarios. So stick your neck out. Speak up when you'd usually keep quiet. Take a new exercise class even though you don't know the moves. Go to that party where you don't know anyone. Practice facing your fears.

- Evaluate and celebrate the end result. When you do take on something that requires a good dose of personal courage, notice that you took a risk and survived. You stood up for something that mattered, and you persisted! Give yourself credit, and know that you can do it again if you have to.

CHAPTER 21

SHOW THAT YOU CARE

Too often we underestimate the power of a touch, a smile,
a kind word, a listening ear, an honest compliment,
or the smallest act of caring,
all of which have the potential to turn a life around.

—Leo Buscaglia

Few leadership skills are as important as showing that you care about your people—not in a perfunctory way, but with genuine concern about their well-being.

As a young leader, I did not understand the importance of showing others that I cared for them. It wasn't that I didn't care, but that I didn't show it. Perception is as good as reality, and I failed to realize that.

As I travel the country teaching, I ask my students to participate in an exercise to help them determine the qualities they deem most important for leaders to demonstrate. I have found it to be a worthwhile exercise, and have received many positive comments from participants. I recommend you also try this.

I instruct each student to write down the names of the five most influential leaders in their life. No particular order is necessary. I then ask them to write down the five worst leaders in their life. An interesting observation from the classroom is that people have no trouble writing down the names of their worst leaders. My students' responses are almost comical. Many smile and say, "Man, that was the worst leader and the worst experience of my life."

After writing down the names of the leaders, both good and bad, I have each person write down the characteristics that warranted the leader's assignment to each list. The qualities for the worst leaders range from stubborn, dishonest, unfair, and unwilling to listen. Not surprisingly, the characteristic most often listed on the worst leader list is the word selfish. Many class participants agree that a boss who is self-centered and did not care about them as a person was the worst kind of leader.

The leadership qualities most mentioned for the best leaders include honesty, integrity, fairness, and good communication. Overwhelmingly, the reason leaders make the *best* list is that the leader cared about them as a person, not just an employee.

Showing that you care about the people you lead is vital, and creates harmony that helps form lasting partnerships, which in turn, can greatly improve the quality of work.

The real purpose of my classroom exercise is to create a personal compass. I try to have my students reflect upon which leadership qualities they should possess, and which ones they should avoid.

Not long after becoming chief of police, I was looking for leadership books that would give me guidance in becoming a better leader. I came across *Winning Every Day* by Lou Holtz, former Notre Dame head football coach. In the book, Coach Holtz asks three simple questions of leaders: Do you care about your people? Can they trust you? Are you committed to excellence?

Unfortunately, I paid more attention to the *Are you committed to excellence?* question than the other two. For years, I focused on improving the organization I was leading through policy improvement, accreditation, and organizational change instead of caring about the people. This was a major mistake. It was only after I focused on caring about the people in the organization first, that I became a better leader.

I can recall a particular moment where showing how much I cared changed a relationship with a subordinate. I had been demanding on a lieutenant that worked as the executive officer. I was constantly demanding the most out of the him, and could clearly see how much leadership potential he possessed. We spent many hours working on projects that saved the city thousands of dollars and manpower. We had a close working relationship, but I'm not sure I conveyed how much he meant to me as a colleague.

When the lieutenant lost one of their parents, I did the perfunctory text message and calls, to show that I cared. But only when I made a personal visit to their home and told them how sorry I was for their loss, did I realize the importance of showing how much you care.

Several months after the funeral, I was sitting in my office and the lieutenant came in and sat. I could tell that he had something on his mind.

He paused for a second, and then and said, "Chief, I didn't realize how much you cared about me. I know we work together every day, but you coming to my house and visiting with my family when my Dad died meant so much to me. I will never forget that."

I learned that hardworking qualities are good for a leader to possess, but folks don't care how smart you are, how hard you work, or what you accomplish, until they understand how much you care about them. How much you cared for them matters most of all. A surprising revelation, but one that improved my leadership.

Over time, I transitioned from being a mission-focused leader to a people-focused leader. And as a result, I became more effective.

Tips for Caring for Employees

- Spend time with them. Spending time not only shows that you care, but it helps build relationships.

- Work on building trust. Trust cannot be overstated. It is the foundation of all relationships, the currency that each of us use to work with each other.

- Show empathy. Empathy is the fastest form of human interaction. No one cares how much you know, until they know how much you care.

CHAPTER 22

GROW FUTURE LEADERS

"You don't own the your leadership position
within an organization, you are only renting it.
The rent you pay are leaders you grow."

—Dean Crisp

One of the most important things a leader should be committed to is growing future leaders. The reality is that you are already doing this, whether you are trying to or not. Leaders have a great deal of influence over those they are in charge of. Helping others grow into good leaders just makes sense.

Think of a leader who has had great influence on you. Most of us may not admit it, but we have become a product of what we observe. We learn by watching others.

You are a reflection of past leaders and their past leaders. Your legacy of leadership will long surpass your career. Every leader influences their followers with their leadership characteristics. These values live on well into the next generations.

I remember being a basketball coach for a Christian school, in my early twenties. I had never been a basketball coach before, but I felt I was up to the challenge. I had no experience to draw upon, other than what I had observed. In high school, our basketball coach was demonstrative and demanding. He would throw towels and stalk up and down the court, ranting and raving. He was a great guy off the court, but he took on a completely different personality when coaching. By watching him, I was influenced that this was the right way to coach basketball. I would bet that he never knew that he had influenced me.

Now, several years later, I was the coach, and I found myself adopting his style. This may not have been a problem in a public school, but I was the coach at a conservative Christian school. During one game, I was ranting and raving on the sidelines and being terribly demanding of a team with great heart, but little talent. Then it dawned on me: I wasn't being myself. Instead, I was emulating what I had learned from my high school coach. I also noticed the kids were not responding like I had hoped. I realized that I had to change my style to best fit this group. But I also learned a great lesson in leadership. We often model the behavior of others, even if it does not fit our personality or style. As leaders, we need to understand our effect on others.

My coaching experience helped me to work harder to understand who I was as a leader, and to develop more suitable skills for those I lead. It also helped me see just how powerful the impact of other leaders can be on us. I was shocked to learn that I was behaving like the coach I had observed years before, even though he was far from my favorite role model.

How many of us understand how important our actions are, and the lasting effect we may have on our followers? If we serve as leaders, we will be role models. This reality places a higher degree of responsibility upon each of us to do the best for our people in all situations, because our actions will last well-beyond the moment at hand. We will grow future leaders regardless of whether we intend to. So why not create the best leaders we can?

Understanding that a major component of being a good leader is to help grow future leaders will help you improve your leadership. It just makes sense. If I embrace the concept that I am helping grow future leaders, then I will be more conscious of my actions—I will consciously strive to be a better example.

In *Peaks and Valleys* by Spencer Johnson, a young man climbs the peaks of life to find an old man who lives there. He asks the old man how to continually live on the peaks of life. The old man only agrees to the younger if he agrees to return to the valleys of life and share his knowledge. The wise old man understands that if he returns and teaches others, it will benefit the young man as much as it benefits the future pupils.

The wise old man was right. If we commit to helping others become better, we will help ourselves become better.

Leaders can choose inspiration or manipulation as the major motivation for getting employees to accomplish a task. Inspiration gets better results and creates more commitment. This takes more time, and is sometimes labor-intensive. But it is worth the effort. Manipulation is effective at times, but requires constant monitoring of the employee, and stunts growth.

No leader owns their position; they are merely renting it. You will one day walk away, and someone else will take over. I think we owe a great deal to those who have entrusted us with leading others. The leaders you create will be the rent you pay to your organization for entrusting you with the position of leadership. A small price for such a major investment.

Tips on Creating Future Leaders

- Focus on growing yourself first.
- Understand your *why* of leadership, and communicate that to those you lead.
- Create a culture of leadership by focusing on the growth of others.
- Create a standard of excellence for those you lead.
- Lead by example.
- Motivate through inspiration, not manipulation.

CHAPTER 23

MENTOR OTHER LEADERS

*A good leader is one who can tell another
how to reach his or her potential;
a great leader is one who can help another
discover this potential for him or herself.*

—Bo Bennett

The word *mentor* has its origins in Greek mythology. When Odysseus left for the Trojan War, he left Mentor in charge of his son, Telemachus. The first published usage of the word *mentor* can be traced back to 1699, in a book titled *Les Aventures de Télémaque*. The modern usage of *mentor* often refers to a trusted friend, counselor, or teacher, usually a more experienced person.

The book *Peaks and Valleys* by Spencer Johnson is about how to live the majority of your life in the peaks and less in the valleys. In the book, a young man climbs to the peaks of life (they are represented by mountains) and finds an old man living at the peak. The old man begins to tell him about living there and how much better it is than living in the valley. He offers to teach the young man how to live there, but he gives him one condition: he must go back to the valley and teaches others what he has learned. The old man understood the importance of mentoring others—a simple condition, but one that required him to find others and to teach them how to live better.

Leaders should strive to be mentors to other leaders. Opportunities to become a mentor present themselves in many ways. Someone is always leading someone else, but both parties in a mentoring relationship will benefit one another. This entire exchange can be tremendously rewarding.

I have had mentors, and I have mentored several police chiefs over the course of my career. Those treasured relationships are still intact today, and I am still learning from them. This is to be distinguished from growing future leaders as discussed in the previous chapter which is often a long-term relationship. Yes, to grow a future leader is to be a mentor, however, mentoring is a role all leaders do all the time in every aspect of a leader's life. As leaders, we can spend so much time growing others, leading the organization, that we don't look to each other for mentorship.

I was struck by an article I read in the *Asheville Citizen Times* newspaper, about Dr. Billy Graham. Although he died several years ago, I recall the article describing his life as an evangelist. Dr. Graham was talking about the importance of having someone he could go to when he was in need of spiritual advice. It amazed me that one of the most influential people on the planet also needed someone to help them. Everyone needs a mentor.

In *Scrambled*, pilot Martin Richard writes about being on the tarmac on September 11, 2001, and being ordered to take flight with the possibility of taking out a plane full of civilians, and the gut-wrenching decision that may lie ahead. He describes how fighter pilots always fly with a wingman. The role of the wingman is to check the surrounding areas that the lead pilot can't see. Richard describes it as checking your six—your back. Mentors, like pilots, can help us check our six.

Being a mentor is not without challenges. Like any relationship, mentoring partnerships require continuous effort to maintain.

I am continually looking for opportunities to mentor others, especially new police chiefs and supervisors. This challenges me to remain current on events and trends in law enforcement and leadership, which makes better equipped to help others.

I consistently mentor former law enforcement employees, students, and even a recent retirees. One of my mentees took a job outside law enforcement, in the security industry. During the first few months, he was questioning his decision to retire and join this industry. As we talked through the decision processes to retire or take his current job, he realized that nothing had changed. Only his anxiety was causing him to question his decisions. After this self-revelation, he settled down and was able to objectively look at his new job with confidence and a positive outlook.

The rule of Thirty-Three-and-One-Third can be applied to mentoring. Most people mistakenly believe mentoring entails an upward or downward dynamic where you help others and others help you. This is true to some extent, but there is much more to the relationship. Mentoring should be an upward, downward, and sideways proposition. Using the One-Third rule, you should choose to spend one-third of your time with people who are above your level of thinking and responsibilities, one-third with those on your level, and one-third with to those below your level.

Think of it like this: if you only mentored people who were below your level, you would be constantly giving and not receiving. This would drain your energy to the point of exhaustion. As a mentor, you also need to be fed and re-energized. Your needs will be nourished by spending time with individuals above or equal to your level.

Tips on Mentoring

- Be willing to learn.
- Be willing to teach.
- Be humble.

- Give as much as you take.
- Seek to get as much as you give.
- Listen first, talk last.
- Remember the One-Third rule—equally dividing your time with those below you, equal to you, and above you.

CHAPTER 24

DON'T HOLD A GRUDGE

There is no evidence that dogs have the kind of
complex emotional lives and value systems that we do.
It's one reason why we love them so much, in fact. They
are neither "good" nor "bad." They don't hold grudges,
act in petty ways, or seek revenge.
They read our moods, but not our minds

—Jon Katz

Grudges are the by-product of anger and the failure to forgive others, and they are almost always destructive. Dr. Phil said, "Forgive others not because they deserve to be forgiven, but because you deserve to be free from them."

Holding grudges generally starts with being judgmental and not giving others the benefit of the doubt. How many times have you walked into a room and immediately began looking at others with a critical eye? Did you ever find yourself looking for faults in how people are dressed, how their hair looks, what colors they are wearing, or maybe just who they are? Many of us begin our judgment of others long before the first words are ever spoken. We judge people according to our own standard of acceptance.

Judging others will keep you angry. Don't automatically assume malice when things do not go your way. I have found that I have a better outlook on life, and I become a much better person, when I withhold judgment.

In today's leadership environment, the people we lead have high expectations. Our reaction to the actions of others can cause a lifetime of pain and anguish. Sometimes we experience emotional pain so terrible that we become emotionally scarred. I have experienced this type of scarring, and have lived with the destructive force that holding a grudge can deliver. I understand how grudges can disrupt and fracture your life. I am guessing many of you have had similar experiences.

One justification for holding a grudge was to protect myself. I thought that if I held a grudge long enough, I could find relief from the pain the person had caused. Boy, was I wrong. The resulting anger gave me short-term relief, but long-term anguish. I had convinced myself that if I remained angry at the person, I did not have to be accountable for the actions that resulted from my anger. I could treat that person any way I wished, and felt justified in doing so.

I was thirteen years old when my parents divorced, which caused much anger to enter my life. I allowed that anger to go unchecked for years, and it evolved into a grudge against my father. I eventually learned that when we hold grudges, it disrupts our life. In fact, we can spend so much of our energy on that grudge that the negative feelings start to control, and even destroy, our quality of life. It is hard to find joy when we are locked into a grudge. Holding a grudge allows other people to steal our happiness, little by little.

On a recent trip, I was looking through the items in my backpack. For some reason, I began thinking about the people who have wronged me throughout my life. As I began to search through the bag, it served as a metaphor for my life. The backpack was stuffed full of things I didn't need, just like my tendency to carry around negative experiences. As I began to empty out the pack, I realized that this was exactly what I needed to do with some of the grudges I was holding against others. With sudden clarity, it occurred to me that if I got rid of them, it would lighten my load. The good news is that, since that day, I regularly try to empty the grudges from my life. In so doing, I have freed myself from the grasp of intolerance.

I often say, "Not forgiving people only ensures that you will carry the negative memories of them most every day." I get a strange look from some people, then a smile. Most people tell me that they had never thought of things that way. Then they laugh and say words to the effect: *If I had known that bit of wisdom, I would have forgiven some people a long time ago.*

Grudges prevent you from moving forward. A good friend of mine told me, "You can't live forward by looking in the rearview mirror of life." He was absolutely right.

Edward Chapman is a former inmate who was exonerated after fourteen years on death row in the North Carolina prison system. During a racial justice rally in Asheville, I heard him say, "I don't hold any grudges...because that doesn't do anything for you. You have to move forward."

How many grudges are you holding on to right now? We can all learn a lot from Mr. Chapman.

Tips for Limiting the Effects of Grudges

- Recognize the long-term negative effect of grudges on your personal health.
- Don't allow anger to fester. Deal with it in a non-emotional way. This is easier said than done.
- Understand that you deserve the peace that will come with forgiveness, maybe even more than the person you are forgiving deserves being forgiven.
- Move on with your life.
- Give folks the benefit of the doubt. This is difficult, but will serve you well.

CHAPTER 25

KNOW THE JANITOR

People who matter are most aware
that everyone else does too.

—Malcolm Forbes

In *West Point Leadership Lessons*, Scott Snair tells a story about a captain who taught a leadership course. On the final exam, the instructor included an unusual question. He asked the students to name two maintenance people who currently worked in their building, and to give every detail they knew about the families of the maintenance persons.

This surprised all the students, and several cadets were incensed that such a question would appear on the leadership final exam. At West Point, cadets are ranked according to their grade point average, and class ranking is crucial. It determines which duty station the cadet will be allowed to select upon graduation.

Several students vehemently protested the question. They demanded for the instructor to explain how knowing the name of maintenance people had anything to do with leadership.

The instructor replied, "Leadership is all about achieving the mission with people. If you don't know the names of the important people who take care of this facility, who make it possible for you to have a roof over your head at this academy, how are you going to interact with the members of your platoon? If you ignore the people you see working here every day, perhaps because you think they are not as important as you are, will you also take your soldiers for granted?"

This captain was absolutely right. It is imperative to know each of the people under your command, and to value them as individuals. In fact, when General Norman Schwarzkopf returned to West Point in 1994, after his resounding victory in Iraq during Operation Desert Storm, the general shared a similar observation with all four thousand cadets. General Schwarzkopf said, "I have seen good leaders stand before a platoon and see it as a platoon. But I have seen the great leaders stand before a platoon and see it as forty-four individuals, each of whom has goals and aspirations, each of whom wants to live, and each of whom wants to do good."

The general knew, from the toughest experiences, that no mission gets accomplished unless the leader has a deep appreciation and reverence for people.

Some managers will say that their organization is too big to get to know all their people. That simply means that they have not tried hard enough or cared enough. Leading larger organizations does present challenges in terms of getting to know all your personnel. But consider this: good people, properly motivated, are the only way that excellent work gets done. Leaders, therefore, must get to know, understand, and consider the human beings who work for them. This is a top priority.

Enlightened leaders will find a way to connect with their people, even if they do not see each worker every day. Seize every opportunity to get to know your people. Whether it is an extended mentoring about career development, or a simple hello in the hallway, every subordinate needs to know that he or she matters to the boss. Ask considerate questions, and listen to the answers.

One basic idea is to make sure that every person under your leadership gets to know their folks, and so on down the line. People do not follow absentee leaders. They follow leaders whom they know and trust. Leadership is a social exchange. People will work harder for someone who genuinely cares about them. If your people do not feel they are getting much from you, they are not likely to give their best effort in return. I found out very early in my career that people don't care how smart you are or how much you know, until they know how much you care about them. The ability to build trusting relationships is a foundational leadership requirement.

While I was a police chief, I made sure I knew everyone in my department—including the janitors, and I would always acknowledge every employee. I tried to recognize everyone, to treat people as equals, and to be aware of their importance. This can be accomplished with simple gestures of stopping to say hello, smiling at employees, and asking them how they and their families are doing. This must be done with sincerity and conviction, but can be extremely difficult to do because a good leader is often in perpetual motion. Not unlike other leaders, your calendar is stacked with responsibilities to chair meetings, to attend public gatherings, to answer complaints, to speak with citizens, and to lead your staff. Still, at every opportunity, and through each subordinate commander, I never forgot that people count!

In the law enforcement world, there is an unwritten divide between two groups of employees. The civilian employees receive too little credit for the outstanding job they do for the department. They have a hard time getting recognized, and are often excluded from decisions. In most police agencies, the bulk of the awards and accolades are bestowed upon the sworn personnel. Civilians are somehow expected to do their jobs for less pay, less attention, and less respect. This *sworn versus civilian* conflict often causes a rift amongst the employees, and because of this the morale of both groups and the overall accomplishments of the entire organization suffer mightily. No matter the rank or position, all employees matter, and their well-being is paramount.

The first step towards making sure all employees feel important is inclusion. This can be accomplished many ways, but communication is the key. Making sure everyone has representation and a voice in key meetings will go a long way toward bridging the gap.

As a leader, it is not that hard to predict where problems are likely to develop, and then to take proactive steps to make sure everyone feels they are valuable members of the team. A capable boss has to make sure that everyone feels important, and that everyone knows you care about them. Don't forget the janitors—you need them. Making sure everyone feels important creates a culture of success.

Tips on How to Connect with Others

- Slow down and realize that connecting with others is the most important thing you will do all day.
- When talking with employees, make eye contact.
- Remember, no one cares how smart you are or how impressed you are with yourself. They care how much you care about them.
- Spread good news.
- Remember, nothing gets done without employees.
- Keep your priorities in order: mission first, people always.
- Every minute spent connecting with employees saves you hours later, trying to motivate them.

CHAPTER 26

PRACTICE UBUNTU

*Sometimes you can't see yourself clearly
until you see yourself through the eyes of others.*

—Ellen DeGeneres

"Ubuntu is a Nguni Bantu term roughly translating to 'human kindness.' It is an idea from the Southern African region which means literally 'humanness,' and is often translated as 'humanity towards others,' but is often used in a more philosophical sense to mean 'the belief in a universal bond of sharing that connects all humanity,'" according to Wikipedia.

Ubuntu states that acknowledging other people is a powerful sign that you recognize they are important and worthwhile. In the Zulu language, the words *Sawa Bona* means *I see you*. This is said when acknowledging someone. In return they say, *Sikhona*, which means *I am here*. The unspoken understanding is that, until you see me, I am not truly here with you.

According to Michael Onyebuchi Eze, a professor of history of African politics at the University of Amsterdam, and author of *the Intellectual History in Contemporary South Africa,* he describes the core of ubuntu as follows:

"[That idea that a] person is a person through other people strikes an affirmation of one's humanity through recognition of an 'other' in his or her uniqueness and difference. It is a demand for a creative intersubjective formation in which the 'other' becomes a mirror (but only a mirror) for my subjectivity. This idealism suggests to us that humanity is not embedded in my person solely as an individual. My humanity is co-substantively bestowed upon the other and me. Humanity is a quality we owe to each other. We create each other and need to sustain this otherness creation. And if we belong to each other, we participate in our creations: we are because you are, and since you are, definitely 'I am.' The 'I am' is not a rigid subject, but a dynamic self-constitution dependent on this otherness creation of relation and distance."

All of us have been on elevators, subways, or in crowds where everyone is in a hurry. Even though we are physically close, we exist in our own worlds, oblivious to others. Think about the awkwardness of getting on a crowded elevator and no one acknowledges each another. The silence is uncomfortable.

Shortly after learning the basic principles of *ubuntu*, I began making a conscious effort to see others and acknowledge their existence. The results have been profound. For instance, I was in an elevator shortly after I decided to practice *ubuntu*. I had entered alone and was riding up several floors. After passing the first few floors, the elevator stopped and a young woman who obviously worked in the building got on. She was carrying several boxes, but was not struggling with them. She seemed content to stand alone, poised and ready to get off at her appointed floor. She stared straight ahead without comment.

I said, "Good morning. My, you look busy today."

She turned around. "Good morning to you. And yes, I am."

I offered to help with the boxes, but she turned down my offer. As we moved past the next few floors, she appeared hesitant to speak.

But then she turned and said, "Thank you for taking the time to speak to me. It is rare that anyone says anything on this elevator. You must be new to the building."

I replied, "Not really. I just thought it was important to acknowledge you this morning."

The look on her face was priceless.

She smiled and said, "Thank you for making my day."

A few moments later, as we arrived at her floor and she was exiting, the woman turned to me and said, "Thanks again."

I was surprised that she was so receptive to my acknowledgment of her. This brief exchange illustrated for me the power of *ubuntu*.

Since then, I have practiced it religiously, and I am always amazed at how well it is received. In fact, I have learned another lesson through *ubuntu*: There is no sweeter sound to people than the sound of their own name. Your friends, your employees, and the people you meet appreciate when you acknowledge them by name. As humans we seek validation, respect, and acceptance.

Enlightened leaders acknowledge and appreciate other people. It does not take much effort to do that. A small exchange of looks and words between two people can be meaningful. As leaders, we sometimes get caught up in the business of our day-to-day challenges—due dates, budgets, crises, personnel decisions, media pressure, and a thousand other emergencies—which can make us socially unaware of the people we come into contact with. But believe me, people notice when you fail to notice them!

I struggled with this problem early in my career. I would be busy with the daily routine, and have minimal time for others. I recall that some of my most painful interactions with others could have been averted if only I had taken the time to acknowledge, connect, and take even a little time with them.

A student in a recent executive class relayed a story that illustrates the importance of recognizing others and respecting them for who they are. I was speaking to a large class of law enforcement professionals all from the same agency. The topic was emotional intelligence and how leaders should be aware of how they present themselves. The student was angry, and I asked them what was wrong.

He said, "I know exactly what you are talking about."

I encouraged him to share his story. He said that when he was a young recruit, he had just completed an especially tough training. He was a member of a state highway patrol agency, and they are known for their tough academies. As a group, his entire class was taken to headquarters to meet the bosses. According to him, the visit was pleasant, and they had met most of the bosses. They were ready to leave the building, and all were standing at attention when the elevator door opened and the colonel walked off. The class recognized the colonel, and they tried their best to look sharp.

The commandant of the school, a seasoned trooper, acknowledged the colonel and said, "Sir, this is the new academy graduating class, and you are scheduled to speak to them tomorrow at their graduation. I would like to introduce them to you. We are proud of them. They have survived a very tough academy, and as you can see, there are only thirty-five left out of the sixty who started."

The colonel looked directly at the commandant and said, "I don't have time to meet the cadets. I am very busy and will see all of them tomorrow."

The student became more upset as he finished the story. He said, "I have never had any respect for that colonel. And to this day, I am still mad and have no use for him."

A simple act of kindness or acknowledgment to the cadets could have made all the difference in the world.

Tips on Incorporating the Spirit of Ubuntu in Your Life

- *See* others.
- Acknowledge people—by name whenever possible.
- Express empathy.
- Ask questions that let them know you were listening.
- Make eye contact.

CHAPTER 27

EXPRESS EMPATHY

Empathy is about standing in someone else's shoes,
feeling with his or her heart, seeing with his or her eyes.
Not only is empathy hard to outsource and automate, but
it makes the world a better place.

—Daniel H. Pink

In *Leadership*, Rudy Giuliani, the former mayor of New York City, states that, "Weddings are optional, but funerals are mandatory." The mayor's point is simple: When your subordinates need you in a time of loss, you must be there.

How often have you had employees or subordinates who lost loved ones? Most leaders simply offer the perfunctory phone call with their condolences. We most often end the call by saying, "Call me if you need anything." Rarely, if ever, does that kind of leader receive a call back. The employee is hurting too much to reach out and ask for help, even if they need it. Of course, the employee will appreciate the call, but nothing beats a personal visit.

Leaders who go the extra mile to attend a wake, a visitation, or a funeral are the kind of leaders who show that their heart is in the game. These leaders demonstrate their willingness to put themselves through emotional turmoil to be available to the employee. At that point, if the employee does need something— such as meeting with a grief counselor, a few days off, or some other accommodation—the employee will likely feel comfortable enough to ask for what they need. Or someone in the family will do it for them. I have seen this happen many times. You can rely upon people to open up; all you have to do is be there.

Even the loss of an employee's pet can devastate them. My career is full of experiences where people were agonized over the death or imminent death of their beloved animal. I learned that if I failed to show sensitivity to their painful emotions, I could lose my emotional bank account with every other pet lover under my command.

I remember an especially poignant time with a former employee. This person had to make a tough decision to euthanize her dog after many years of taking care of the animal. She called me and informed me that she had decided to proceed with the euthanasia, but she also shared that she was having a rough time. So I drove to her house, and got there just as the veterinarian arrived. The employee was indeed having a difficult time.

I watched as the vet injected the dog, and as the animal took its last breath. My employee's emotions were raw, and I let her know that she was not alone, and that all of us at the police department understood her pain.

According to Stephen Covey, "Empathy is the fastest form of human interaction and communication." He is correct. Expressing empathy does not take a great deal of time, but it cannot be faked. Each time I have expressed empathy toward employees, the emotional bonds between us have grown stronger.

I attended FBI National Academy class, session 172, in Quantico, Virginia. The people who attend this training are high-ranking law enforcement professionals from across the nation, and even a few from around the world. A classmate was reminiscing about how a supervisor he had worked for years prior, had shown empathy toward him. My classmate described a time when his father was ill. The father lived approximately nine hours away, in another state. The classmate recalled how there was one particular sergeant that he did not have a great relationship with. They were not open enemies, but they merely coexisted and did not know each other well.

One day, my classmate told the sergeant about his father's severe illness. He mentioned how difficult it was to split his time and attention between his dad's needs and his duties as a patrol cop. Surprisingly, the sergeant expressed sincere sorrow. He advised my classmate to take as much time as necessary to take care of his dad. The sergeant realized that nine-hour drives coupled with the emotional drain of seeing my classmate seeing his dad fade, all added up to an officer who would not be fit to do his duties or safely support his partners at work.

The illness went on for about six more months, until my classmate's father passed away. The sergeant was again thoughtful. He gave my classmate all the time off he needed to be with the family and to make funeral arrangements.

As I heard this story, I thought, This is a solid example of how good leaders take care of their people's needs.

Then my classmate got to the real heart of the matter. What impressed him most about this ordeal was what happened when the funeral was in progress. As he and his family arrived at the cemetery, my classmate saw a lone figure standing on the hill next to the gravesite. My classmate did not pay much attention to the person. He figured it was some friend of his dad's, who my classmate likely didn't know. But as he got closer, he realized it was his own sergeant. The police office was shocked to see him, especially since the two had never been close. As the services began, my classmate began thinking about how the sergeant had driven nine hours, across state boundaries, just to be there for him. There stood the sergeant in full uniform, silent, at attention, giving strength and solace by his presence alone.

As the graveside service ended, my friend began to walk back to the family car. The sergeant met him and shared his condolences.

Mostly, the sergeant wanted to emphasize that whatever happens to one member of the police family, happens to us all. He made clear that whatever time my classmate needed to recover, the time was his and the job would be waiting. He told him, "Just come back when you are ready. We will be waiting on you."

My classmate's opinion of that sergeant would never be the same, and it is a leadership lesson he shares today with all who will listen. He told me that he learned more about leadership from the actions of that sergeant than he had in his entire life.

The amount of energy you put forth with your empathy will have a direct impact on how well the empathy is received and how it is accepted. If you simply send a text to tell someone you are thinking of them, when you should have visited in-person, you will dilute the impact of your empathy, and perhaps even damage your relationship. Although texting has become an accepted form of communication, it is not recommended to replace personal contact.

Remember, no one takes roll at a funeral, but no one ever forgets who doesn't show up.

Tips for Expressing Empathy

- Make sure you truly know what the grieving person is going through. Don't assume you know. Take time to listen to them and find out the depth of their pain and loss.

- Feel what they feel. The only way you can do this is to spend time with them. Experiencing their pain can only be felt if you visit and talk to them. Feeling what they feel will open your eyes to their pain.

- Do what they ask of you to help them through their situation. Offer tangible support, such as time off, or help with meals and errands.

- Energy and empathy go hand in hand. Your empathy will always be judged by the amount of energy you extend. Writing a text is low energy. Making a phone call requires more energy. And a visit, by far, requires the most energy. The degree to which people feel your empathy directly correlates to how much energy you direct toward them when they are grieving.

III
LEADING
ORGANIZATIONS

Leading an organization is not all about leading a process or leading a name or a brand. It's about leading people. In this third and final section, I will provide a framework for leading organizations from the front.

The organizational well-being is the task of the leader, and few, if any, organizations thrive from poor leadership. Studies have consistently shown that organizations that prioritize leadership have consistently outperformed those who do not. In fact, most Fortune 500 companies have a strategic process for identifying and developing their leadership talent. If your organization isn't doing this, it should.

Organizational life today is often complex and filled with miscommunication, hurt feelings, hostility, and a lack of motivation. This doesn't mean that organizations are not productive and able to work through these issues, but it does create a challenging environment for leadership, and is symptomatic of leaders not focused on their people.

Leaders must be at their best every day. They must focus on developing their people and viewing their organization as organic. Organizations are living, breathing things made of people, first and foremost. Leaders who understand this, and understand how to convey the *why* of their organization, will have the most success in today's environment.

In this section, I offer my Diamond Leadership Model as the most effective way to create the synergy that makes organizations successful. As a leader, it is your responsibility to understand your *why* of leadership, how it is tied to the organization's mission, and to effectively convey it to your people. If they know the *why*, the *what* has options.

CHAPTER 28

THE DIAMOND LEADERSHIP MODEL

*Coming together is a beginning,
staying together is progress, and
working together is success.*

—Henry Ford

The ultimate goal of any leader should be to create partnerships with their employees that lead to the desired outcome: synergy. To this end, I've developed a leadership model that shows how a leader can maximize the effectiveness of their people and their organization.

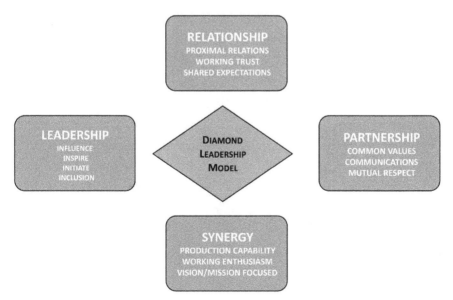

The first prong of this model is Leadership. It is evaluated by using four components: influence, inspire, initiative, and inclusion. These four components are at the core of leadership.

First and foremost, leaders are in the business of influencing others, and they are constantly striving toward the most effective way to get employees to follow and act in a manner consistent with the mission or task. They do this through various methods of persuasion. Some choose to influence others through manipulation—the carrot-and-stick method. But the most effective leaders are able to inspire. The leader that manipulates to gain influence does so because they lack the ability or understanding of how to inspire.

Second, and closely aligned with influence, is a leader's ability to *inspire* employees to perform their best, and to produce results that are reflective of the organization's values and goals. Inspiring employees requires the ability to convey the *why* of the your personal leadership, and the *why* of the organization.

In *Start With Why*, Simon Sinek articulates this perfectly when describing the importance of *why*. "People don't buy what you do. They buy why you do it!"

It's the same with leadership. If those you lead understand your leadership *why*, as well as the *why* of the organization, they will be more inspired to do their job.

The third component of Leadership is *initiative*. Getting employees to take initiative, self-reflect, and always do their best is the primary objective of leaders. Most leaders are actually promoted or selected for their ability to get things done—to take initiative.

Inclusion in today's workplace is absolutely imperative and is why it is the fourth evaluator of the Leadership facet of the Diamond Model. Most people want to be part of a team. The youngest generation of employees is much more likely to produce at the highest levels if inclusion is the rule instead of the exception.

This does not mean just demographically, but also inclusivity of ideas and perspectives. As a leader, being inclusive means you are able to get a variety of viewpoints from your employees, which will build their confidence in your leadership decisions, and create buy-in to the overall goals.

Understanding where you are in each of these four aspects of Leadership allows you develop a plan that will not only improve your leadership, but also the leadership qualities of those who work for you.

Relationship is important personally, and is paramount within organizations, It is the second facet of my Diamond Leadership Model.

The Relationship facet can be developed through three key activities: proximal relations, working trust, and shared expectations. Let's take a look at each of these.

Proximal Relations is time spent with one another. In romance, we would call this *dating*. A professional relationship is similar, without the romantic aspect. As you go to lunch with employees, develop a project with them, you begin to understand what makes each person tick; what makes them laugh and what makes them react positively or negatively to organizational goals.

Only by spending time with someone can you understand how to develop our next aspect: *working trust*. Trust is the foundation of any relationship. You are acting on faith that your coworker will have your back, just as you trust your spouse to remain faithful to the shared goals you have set as a couple. Trust does not happen overnight. In fact, depending on the people involved, it can take months, or even years. Trust develops when promises are kept consistently. Consistency of behavior, constancy of results, and commitment to the goals are all part of establishing working trust with another.

When Relationship has been established, you can then proceed to the next facet of the Diamond Model: Partnership.

Partnerships are vital to organizations. I have found that most employees seek ways to become more involved, and desire active partnership in the decision-making.

Developing partnerships is possible by sharing common values, having effective and meaningful communication, and through mutual respect. With today's employees, developing partnerships is paramount to the success of any leader. Let's take a deeper look at each aspect.

Common values are things you believe important to the way you live and work. They help determine our priorities, and often help us evaluate how our outcomes, both personally and professionally, are manifesting. Just as it would be difficult to be married to someone that did not share your values, it would be hard to have a working partnership with someone who did not share your work ethic, commitment to the job, or dedication to the outcome.

Communication is how we determine what others are all about. Talking through our ideas, beliefs, and views on a project or work problem enables us to evaluate whether we share another's values, and whether we can develop a mutual respect. The ability and willingness to communicate is critical to establishing the rapport needed to create partnership.

If you have communicated well, established the common values you have for the work at hand, the third aspect of creating a partnership usually develops: *mutual respect.*

Mutual respect is born out of authentic communication, which allows people to discover common values that they respect in each other. So as a leader, you may think you are a great communicator, but you may not trust some of your employees to accomplish tasks. This is likely due to an inability to understand or find common values with those people, or to find a respect for the differences of the other.

Synergy is the fourth facet of the Diamond Leadership Model. It is the result of leadership using relationships to form partnerships. Synergy is a union of commonality that creates a workplace full of energy and enthusiasm laden with the potential for increased productivity results.

Working enthusiasm comes easily when employees feel valued because they have a solid relationship with their leader and with their coworkers; and when each employee is clear on the organizational mission. When this occurs, employees feel empowered to solve problems and be creative, because they know those actions are in line with the mission and values of the organization. No need to go ask for permission, or to complain, the synergistic workplace figures it out and creates a better solution than could have been imagined by just one leader. When synergy is created, magical things begin happen in the workplace.

Developing a partnership with today's employees is paramount to the success of any leader. We cannot do this unless we first build a relationship. Sometimes even our best advice goes unappreciated. Every leader has faced the frustration of seeing people ignore our guidance, even though we are certain that our counsel is in their best interest. Often, our employees, or even members of our family, are stuck in a rut and not willing to make the changes that will improve their situation. As the old saying goes, *You can lead the horse to water, but you can't make it drink.*

What causes this? Well, before you go blaming your stubborn or lazy employee, or your obstinate child, there might be a lot more to the story. The inaction and lack of enthusiastic participation you are witnessing could be from the leader's failure to develop a leader-partner relationship. Why should anybody follow your guidance if they don't trust you, know who you are, or believe in what you stand for?

As a leader, I am the most effective when I clearly understand that a partnership cannot exist without first developing a relationship. This partnership occurs only when both parties trust each other and share the same core values.

In every relationship, the parties involved need to establish trust established, or there the relationship will not last. Second, the partners need to share the same principles. Partners can have different opinions on everything from politics to policies, but their core values must be rooted in honesty, integrity, and character. If one person has a different value system than the other, that pairing cannot ever hope to attain an beneficial partnership.

Before you think I am digressing into the connective side of life, please let me explain. It takes a true leader-partner relationship to achieve the kind of communication and buy-in that will allow both parties to listen and act upon each other's suggestions. This certainly applies to romance, but also to work, family, friends, and neighbors. Once a true relationship and partnership is in full swing, it can lead to top development and performance. It takes that kind of trusting partnership to achieve greatness as a team.

Leaders must create an environment that promotes relationships by establishing communication channels. It is what makes you an effective leader. One way to create the appropriate environment is to constantly remind yourself that your primary role as a leader is to create other leaders. When developing relationships with all the people we guide, we will naturally have closer connections with some than others, but without some form of relationship, followers will never adopt the leader's message. They may even be hesitant to share their ideas, or to constructively evaluate yours.

We know relationships take time to develop, but they also take more than just the passage of time. People can grow apart as often as they grow together. You need a clear and collective commitment to communicate and to develop the strength and subtleties of the partnership. Of course, it also helps if you start to formulate some goals.

I have seen leaders push and pull subordinates without understanding that it is the subordinate can chose whether to accept or reject the leader's guidance. People are not marionettes. Each has their own opinions, preferences, fears, talents, and challenges. They will do what they want. So the leader's job is to encourage the follower to do the right things in the right way. Therefore, it is through relationships, not directives, that leaders truly provide direction.

Through partnerships, trust, and values, people will follow. Subordinates are not minions assigned to do your bidding. Only a shallow manager can't see this. Supervisors who think only of reaching their goals cannot see that every goal is accomplished through people. These type of bosses go through life not only unaware of the potential in those they lead, but also their own. Along the way, these managers do not accomplish much, because whatever they do, they do it alone.

People may go through the motions to obey a boss's orders as long as the boss keeps them under constant observation. These employees eventually become disgruntled either from a harmful occurrence, or from a thousand psychological cuts inflicted by uncaring and disconnected supervisors.

Leadership is like teaching. In teaching, we are responsible for facilitating the information and offering it up for the students to absorb. In leadership, we are responsible for initiating relationships and building trusting partnerships, then offering up a mission to achieve—together.

In the article "Managerial Style as a Behavioral Predictor of Organizational Climate," the authors state: "Roughly 53 to 72 percent of how employees perceive their organization's climate can be traced to the actions of one person: the leader. More than anyone else, the boss creates the conditions that directly determine people's ability to work well."

Can leaders who have been in positions for years learn new ways to improve their behavior, relationships, and results? Can an old dog learn new tricks? In *Primal Leadership*, Daniel Goleman states that according to research findings, even the most senior leaders can improve their leadership if they have the desire to do so. Leaders can, and do, make significant, and even life-altering, improvements in their management styles. Done right, these leadership enhancements create a ripple effect within their entire organization. They accomplish the mission through relationships with people.

The Desired End Result Is Synergy

Synergy is the result of leadership, relationship, and partnership. It can be defined as: working together and producing desired results for a common purpose.

An example of synergy is when a symphony orchestra is performing in perfect harmony, with each member playing their part to achieve the desired sound.

Have you ever worked on an assignment where everyone was excited and had plenty of enthusiasm and energy? Everyone looked forward to coming to work, and time seemed to fly by. I have worked in a synergistic environment, and the amount of work we accomplished was amazing.

One example was the Special Response Team that I lead. This is a group of highly trained individuals who take on specific assignments that normal patrol is not equipped to deal with. We always came to work prepared and motivated. Our team had a motto: All Heart, All Effort, and 100% Voluntary. This is the effect synergy can have on a group.

Synergy, as Stephen Covey says in *The 7 Habits of Highly Effective People*, is 1+1= 3, not 2. He explains that when we get together, we combine my idea with your idea and come up with a third alternative that is better than either of the individual ideas.

Synergy is a major force multiplier, and this model of creating partnerships encourages teamwork and buy-in.

Synergy means being in sync with those around you. Psychologically, we all need harmony. Harmony at work, home, school, and with friends is the key to happiness. Think about it. When you are in harmony with those around you, you feel energized and motivated. Synergy is the key to harmony.

Using the Diamond Model as the foundation of your leadership can improve you, as well as those you lead. It will not be easy to implement this model at first. It will take a great deal of work, but it will be worth the effort.

Using this model as the foundation to my leadership made me a better leader, mentor, and partner. We can never accomplish great things by ourselves. Greatness will always require the cooperation of others, and this model will help you achieve that cooperation.

In order to help you grow your leadership toward synergy, I am offering you the opportunity to take a free Diamond Leadership Model Assessment, at www.lhln.org. I caution you to be in the right mindset and to be fully honest with yourself as you respond to the questions. Only through honest self-reflection can you begin to see where you need to grow your leadership. There are no right or wrong answers, and the test will reveal the areas you need to focus on to develop your leadership skills.

Tips for Implementing the Diamond Leadership Model

- Start with your *why* of leadership. If you use that as the base of all you do, it will inform your implementation of the Diamond Leadership Model.

- Relationships are the foundation of the model. Get to know your people. Understand what motivates each of them.

- Allow your people to fail. In order for them to grow, you must step back and allow failure. Being open-minded is critical to success.

- Be available to coach and mentor.

CHAPTER 29

DO RIGHT

*Leadership consists not in degrees of technique,
but in traits of character; it requires moral rather than
athletic or intellectual effort, and it imposes on both
leader and follower alike the burdens of self-restraint.*

—Lewis H. Lapham

Having been promoted to chief early in my career, there were many times when I would struggle with tough decisions. Being an avid reader, a mentor of mine recommended a book written by Lou Holtz, entitled *Winning Every Day*. In it, Coach Holtz outlined three rules to consider when faced with difficult decisions. I have found these to be useful. But over time, I added a fourth rule.

The do-right rules

1. Do the right thing
2. For the right reason
3. At the right time
4. In the right way.

Doing the right thing is often challenging. Leaders face tough decisions on a daily basis, and knowing what's right is often difficult to discern because of the many unintended consequences surrounding a possible decision.

I recall a conversation I had with a newly elected county sheriff shortly after he was sworn in. We were discussing how he had made some challenging decisions in the past, and he said, "Doing the right thing is always easy."

I was surprised by his statement, but I waited for him to finish before asking why he thought doing the right thing was easy.

He replied, "It just is."

I thought back to all the times I had made tough decisions, and how my courage was often tested during the decision-making process.

I replied, "Sheriff, doing the right thing is often difficult."

He paused and thought for a moment. The said, "Please explain."

I told the him that in my years of decision-making, I found it difficult to do the right thing all the time. I went on to explain that every decision impacts people, yet the personal interests of all the people surrounding those decisions are often in conflict with each other. Simply stated, if you please one person, the other will be unhappy, and so forth. I went on to say that what I generally do is consider everyone's input and the potential impacts, but I ultimately choose what I feel is best. Those decisions always factored in the impact on the organization and our ability to achieve our goals. Naturally, there would be a number of people who would disagree. But effective leaders make decisions that are in the best interest of the team and the organization. Unfortunately, this often conflicts with the personal interests of individuals.

The sheriff replied, "I see. Let me get this straight. Doing the right thing can be difficult?"

"Exactly," I replied.

He smiled and said, "OK, so when does the hard part come?"

Realizing he had only been the leader of the organization for about twenty-four hours, I knew this sheriff was short on experience, but long on enthusiasm.

I said, "Sheriff, let's do this. In six months, you call me, and we will have this conversation again."

He agreed, and we left it at that.

A few months after that conversation, I received a call from that same sheriff.

He said, "Dean, you were right. Doing the right thing can be really tough. The past few months have been a whirlwind. Everybody who works for me, and everyone who says they voted for me, wants something. I mean, it is amazing how many times a day I have to say no to someone. I am constantly balancing what is right for the organization with the personal interests of our employees and our public. Man, this is no fun."

The sheriff went on to tell me about some of the hard decisions he had made regarding transfers and promotions. I sensed that he now had a thorough understanding of how tough it was to always do the right thing. But I never said I told you so; I didn't have to.

The second do-right rule, *doing things for the right reason*, refers to the ability to justify the *why* of your decision. Is it being made for the right reason? Is it in the best interest of the organization? And does this decision coincide with our mission and values?

Leadership decisions can appear to conflict with individual interests, in pursuit of team interests. This is easier to understand if we understand that most organizations are separated into three components: the individual, the team, and the organization. Each component plays a particular role to the success of the organization.

Individual refers to persons working in the organization and what value they contribute. Of course, self-interest needs to be considered, and how people will respond to the reason.

Team refers to work groups, divisions, or sections to which these persons are assigned. I have often found that individual interests are in conflict with the team. In today's world, the word *team* is ubiquitous.

Organization refers to everyone. Leaders can make individual or team decisions for the right reason, but they may still conflict with the organization. Keeping these components in mind when explaining the right reason is important.

The *right time* refers to implementation of a decision according to the timeframe when it has the best chance for success. I remember working with a bright and charismatic sheriff who was concerned about the timing of all decisions. Being young and aggressive, I would often come up with what I considered to be good ideas for improvement. He would always say, "Yes, that idea is good, and it will probably work. But it will work better when the timing is right." I can still hear his words in my head: "Timing is everything. I would rather make a good decision at the right time, than a great one at the wrong time."

The more I think about his advice on timing, the more I understand just how right he was.

I can remember working on my master's degree in public administration and taking a course in public policy. The subject matter was timing and acceptance of public policy. One of the most important points was that any public policy must have a softening period before it is fully accepted.

If the timing of our decisions is not right, the softening period will be adversely effected, and acceptance may never take place.

The last component, *making decisions the right way*, is critical to the success of our decisions. Doing the right thing, for the right reason, at the right time can all be negated by not doing it the right way.

Doing it the right way will always help mitigate the pain of hard decisions, and over the course of my thirty-year career, I have seen many examples of this. For example, a police agency can promote the right person to a higher rank for all the right reasons. But if that promotion is not accomplished in the right way, their can be a negative impact on the individual, the organization, or both. I have seen leaders of organizations skew promotional processes in favor of certain people by writing the qualifications for the position to fit only their choice. This is certainly not the right way to promote someone.

The way we do things matters. How we reach our decisions and implement them can be for naught if we fail to do it the right way. Our approach to and implementation of discipline is another example of how we can make damaging errors if we don't impose discipline in the right way.

Much of discipline is handed out the wrong way and with the wrong approach. Many leaders approach discipline with a win-lose attitude. This is a simplistic approach used many times for the leader's own expediency and convenience. It is as simple as this: I am the leader; do what I say. You are the follower; I win, and you lose.

I have witnessed many encounters like this. For example: The follower is late for work or seems to be having some minor problems at work. The leader calls the follower in for a counseling session, and says, "I've noticed you have been late to work on several occasions, and seem to be having some performance issues. If this does not get corrected, I will have to take it to the next level. The result will be harsher punishment, and even termination, if you do not correct this immediately."

The follower in this situation had no opportunity to offer reasons or mitigations for the problem. With this approach, the leader apparently wins and the follower loses.

The leader in this situation may have had good intentions, but the discipline was not done the right way. The truth is, the leader just suffered a great loss. The approach described above is likely to result in minimal, if any, employee loyalty to the organization, and certainly none for leader. This approach may correct the employee's behavior in the short-term, but most often does not improve the long-term performance.

In the example, if the leader had chosen to find out what was causing the employee to be late, the result would have been an improved relationships between leader and follower.

Doing things the right way is definitely the right choice.

Tips for Doing it Right

- Let your emotions settle before acting.
- Break the problem down into small pieces.
- Imagine all possible outcomes.
- Find someone to share your thoughts with.
- Consider the impact of your decisions on others.
- Use experience as a guide.

CHAPTER 30

THREE S'S TO KNOW
WHEN IT'S TIME TO MOVE

In other words, don't expect to always be great.
Disappointments, failures and setbacks are a normal part
of the lifecycle of a unit or a company,
and what the leader has to do is constantly be up and say,
"We have a problem. Let's go and get it."

—Colin Powell

Leadership is, no doubt, a tough business. I have had a number of conversations about how difficult it is to be a good leader, let alone to try to be a great leader.

Being a leader requires personal and professional sacrifice. Like all things, there is a time and a season for everything. Leadership is no different. Leaders make a multitude of difficult decisions on a daily basis. Many are related to day-to-day affairs (the whirlwind), and others are about the past, present, and future of the organization.

There are three major decisions that are at the core of a leader which are: when to begin, when to stay, and when to leave. For me, the decision to stay was the easiest. The decision to leave was the hardest.

I have seen many leaders outstay their welcome, exceeding their ability to be effective. Many either don't know, or they refuse to admit, when it is time to go. But leaders must know and recognize when it's time to pass the torch.

Using the three S's—sacrifice, service, and suffering—I have created a way to help you determine when the time is right to make a career move. This will hopefully help you avoid making emotional decisions that can be detrimental to your career. The three S's are simple, and each S describes your current mindset as a leader.

Sacrifice, the foundation of the three, represents what every good leader does daily. They put the needs of others before their own. Any good leader will always take care of their people first. Simon Sinek articulates this well in *Leaders Eat Last*. Sinek describes what he learned from the military: If you make sure your people are taken care of—in regard to supplies, food, sleep— they will take care of the mission.

Service refers to your perspective on leadership. Leaders are there to serve the people. A good way to describe this is *servant leadership*. It means that you as a leader are committed to serving, not being served. Mindset is key to servant leadership. A leader can either look inward, making sure all of their needs are met; or outward, making sure all their people are taken care of first. An outward mindset is key when it comes to service.

Suffering is the anti-service mindset. If you have never suffered as a leader, then you have never led people. Leading and suffering go hand in hand. How many times have you had to do something you did not want to do, or make a tough decision that had major consequences for everyone? How many hours have you spent on the phone or answering e-mails at midnight, or missed a family event because work came first? Or have you felt that you have taken your organization as far as you could, and you have become complacent? When leading becomes more about suffering, and becomes too much to bear, then it is time to consider moving on.

I can attest to this value of the three S test. Because my suffering far out-weighed my service, I decided that it was time to move on and let someone else lead the way. The formula is a solid way to evaluate where you are.

The 3 S's of Deciding to Make a Move

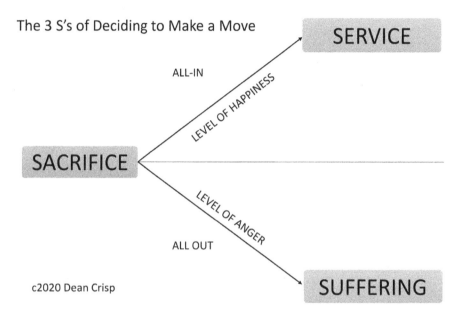

c2020 Dean Crisp

Looking at this image, you see that the middle S is *sacrifice*, and at the top are the words *All In*. This represents the feeling you experience when your leadership is all about service. The top S is *service*, and the bottom one is *suffering*. The upward trajectory of service is on purpose because it represents how we feel when we are in a position where our service far outweighs any suffering we may be experiencing.

Suffering is purposely located at the bottom because it represents a downward trajectory of not only our mindset, but of the negative feelings we may be experiencing.

Both *happy* and *anger* are located on the drawing to indicate what we experience as we begin to drift into those areas.

SOS is the common signal for help. I use it to show that the further we travel downward in the drawing, the more we begin seeking help by either leaving, or hoping someone will come to our rescue.

We will fluctuate on the chart according to the daily, weekly, and monthly issues we face as a leader. It is only when we begin to trend downward, or begin to realize that sacrifice is not worth the suffering anymore, that we must begin to make an exit strategy. Leaving on time is a key to sustaining an intact legacy, emotional survival, and organizational welfare.

Tips for Using the Three S Model

- Don't wait until you are at the low end of the S's before you realize you have to make adjustments. Then, it may be too late.

- Understand your *why*.

- Your *why* is usually your prime motivation. Understand that your time is limited in leadership. It happens to all of us. When your time comes, make a change. Staying longer will only make things worse.

CHAPTER 31

ESTABLISH A CLEAR VISION

Where there is no vision, there is no hope.

—George Washington Carver

Leaders create a sustainable followership by establishing a clear, viable vision.

T.E. Dow Jr. describes vision as a revolutionary image in his *Sociological Quarterly* (1969) article entitled, "The Theory of Charisma." Dow writes that vision "acts not only as the catalyst for change, but also as the organization's bedrock, keeping it moving forward despite obstacles and challenges, transforming purpose into action."

A successful vision must attract commitment and inspire enthusiasm, create meaning by clarifying purpose and direction, establish a standard of excellence, and bridge the present and future. Simultaneously, a leader's vision must consider the follower's needs, values, and hopes. The vision must also instill self-confidence that will translate into a state of empowerment.

One of the most important tasks of any leader is to create a world that does not currently exist. Now that may seem impossible, but understand that *vision* is the future state of things. People want to know where they are headed, and they won't simply *get on board* if they don't know the destination. Leaders can create a clear vision by working with their employees to gain acceptance. Without the support of their followers, leaders won't be successful.

The importance of having a clear vision cannot be overstated. The word *vision* describes a future point that will make the organization better. Working for an organization that has no clear vision is like being in a hurry to nowhere.

Early in my career, I worked for an agency where the leaders had no clear vision. Every day we repeated the same things as we did the day before, which created an environment of mediocrity. No one knew where we were going. Thus, stagnation and malaise set in. Complaints and discord became the norm. Morale was low, and hope for a better future was non-existent. This eventually led to the downfall of all of our top leaders.

After new leadership came on board, things quickly changed when they articulated a vision for our agency. Performance improved, and morale was high, all because people had a clear idea of where we they were headed. It was amazing to see the transformation. I learned a valuable lesson on how important it is to know where you're going, not only for me, but for the entire organization.

Our personal vision of where we're going is exactly like our organizational one. If we don't know where we are going, any road will take us there.

Creating a vision for others to follow can be a difficult task, but it is one of the most important aspects of leadership. Let's take a practical look at vision. It is not as simple as deciding where to go for lunch, but the example can give you perspective on the importance of vision.

Imagine that you are going to lunch with a few colleagues, and you get into the car without deciding on where to go. I have done this hundreds of times. Someone says, "Where are we going?" and the common reply is "I don't care." Then someone says, "Me either."

Until someone provides the lunch option, you are sitting in the parking lot, or driving with no direction. Eventually, you all of you end up at the agreed-upon location. Just a few minutes ago, no one knew where you were going, but because someone provided the suggestion—or vision—now everyone is focused on enjoying lunch.

In *The 7 Habits of Highly Effective People,* Stephen Covey says that before we create anything in the physical, we must first create it in our minds.

When you have a clear vision, be sure to explain it to your subordinates. Just having the vision is not enough. Everyone that you're leading should understand your vision for the short- and long-term direction of the organization. Not only should they know, but they should also articulate this vision on a daily basis to reinforce its importance. Through repetition, the vision becomes clear, and the employees are more likely to buy into the vision, as well as work on behalf of the leader's directions.

Promoting a clear vision requires dynamic engagement between the leaders and members of their organization. Many leaders believe that posting their vision on the wall will create buy-in. It does not. It will soon become invisible to most, noticeable only when someone new sees it.

Leaders must articulate their vision on a daily basis and keep it front and center of all their actions. Only then will employees begin to see it as the leader does, and embrace it.

Tips for Creating a Vision

- First, know where you are.
- Don't let the past overly influence your future. Yes, learn from it, but don't let the fear of it stop you.
- Make the vision clear, precise, and easy to understand. *Being better* is not a clear vision. For examples, please see the Resources page on our website, www.lhln.org.

- Seek input from those who will be affected.
- Develop a clear strategy to achieve your vision.
- Refer to your vision frequently so everyone will understand the importance.
- Make the vision actionable and doable.
- Encourage others to buy-in.

CHAPTER 32

AS A LEADER YOU MUST ACT LIKE ONE

The leader can never close the gap between himself and
the group. If he does, he is no longer what he must be. He
must walk a tightrope between the consent he must win
and the control he must exert.

—Vince Lombardi

Leaders must resist becoming too friendly with those they lead to prevent a misunderstanding of how the relationship, trust, and respect should co-exist in the workplace.

When I was a young cop, one of my training officers gave some important advice. He said, "You can't drink with your friends on Friday night, and then arrest them on Saturday night when you come to work."

You must rise above the group and separate yourself. Not in a haughty way, but a way in which they understand that as a leader, you now represent the organization.

Working trust is an essential factor in developing relationships. The leader must establish clear lines of positional and professional authority that are never crossed, and are to be respected at all times. This is not only true with authority, but also with attitudes and approaches toward leadership. Simply put, as leaders, we have a choice. You can choose to remain above the fray, with a positive attitude that creates partnerships. Or you can choose to take part in group think, and be a part of the naysayers with a counterproductive attitude that causes dissension.

As a leader, you must stay focused and understand that your role as a leader is to represent the organization and the other leaders. You cannot accomplish this if the troops do not understand that you have drawn a clear line of responsibility.

As leaders, we have the responsibility to motivate others in a positive manner reflective of our organizational values. This responsibility is corrupted by believing that we can still be one of the gang and remain involved in inappropriate conduct such as complaining or gossiping.

Do you let others influence you to the point where your own words and actions are subverted? Do you start to take on the negative habits of those you are supposed to be leading? The choice is clear, and it is related to strength of character, to being grounded in deep and meaningful principles.

How many of us have heard our parents say, "Just because your friends are doing it, doesn't mean you have to do it." Our parents were onto something big. Humans are social animals. As a result, we cannot help but to be influenced by our interactions. The influence of others upon us is real, and he effects cannot be downplayed.

Unscrupulous people are hypermotivated. They are determined to find allies who will participate in their way of thinking and acting. Many people are willing to follow bad examples because they lack the strength to resist. I guess it is easier to take the path of least resistance, and that path often leads to lazy and self-centered goals.

We have all seen news footage of officers, sergeants, and chiefs sacrificing their ethics in one form or another. Leaders must make tough choices, and the first one is to recognize that you are not one of the troops anymore.

I have written this book largely from a law enforcement perspective because I think it shows strong examples of heroism and meaningful human interaction. It also points clearly to what can go wrong. Even if your world is banking, selling, teaching, or social work, be mindful of the stories you have seen on the news where cops have stolen, used excessive force, practiced racism, or otherwise lost touch with their integrity. Remember, police officers are screened by an aggressive and thorough background process. Police agencies investigate their finances, personal choices, school grades, relationships, and much more before they ever get hired. We conduct polygraph tests, drug tests, and psychological profiles as added confirmation. So if these apparently good people can commit crimes, what does that say for the rest of us.

Remember the exercise I have students do in my leadership classes of listing the five traits of good and bad leaders they have had? Remember how easy it was for them to list the abysmal ones first? The overwhelming answer is that the students clearly remembered leaders who had the most negative effect on them, which shows the strong influence that negative behavior has on our mind. It is difficult to let go, and therein lies its power.

As a leader, we must be careful not to let the negative behaviors of others influence our mindset. If we let their influence count for more than our own integrity, we begin to slide down the infamous slippery slope. This slide can land us in a position where we become *them* much more than they become us.

If we follow leaders with the right stuff, their influence is highly constructive. Be wary, however, of the detrimental leaders who are present at all levels of society, and likely within in your own organization. Given the slightest opportunity, these malevolent leaders will exert a corrupt influence to invade the mindset of other people in your company, perhaps even you.

This wicked influence is always out there just waiting to ruin the careers and the reputation of leaders at all levels. At a minimum, morally deficient people will damage productivity and collegial cooperation. They will take people away from you, and the common good, creating dreadful organizational problems in the process.

To combat this, we leaders need to be strong role models. We need to be the source of positive influence, not the recipients of bad advice, thereby making us leaders worthy of following.

Tips for Acting Like a Leader

- Remember that as a leader, you represent the organization.
- Don't complain to subordinates.
- Create a strong leadership foundation with your subordinates by embracing the concepts of the Diamond Leadership Model.
- Be courageous to stop bad behavior. Silence makes you complicit.
- Create an environment of professionalism.

CHAPTER 33

EMBRACE DIVERSITY

We need to give each other the space to grow,
to be ourselves, to exercise our diversity.
We need to give each other space so that we may both
give and receive such beautiful things as ideas, openness,
dignity, joy, healing, and inclusion.

—Max de Pree

Diversity is not about giving special privileges to individuals based on their race, gender, or religion. Diversity is about inclusion. Diversity ensures the opportunity for meaningful participation by everyone, resulting in a more complex, more comprehensive work product. It means giving consideration and respect. It means acknowledging human dignity with the intention of leaving no one behind.

In the twenty-first century, diversity is a requirement for any organization that is committed to excellence and concerned with employee satisfaction. Gone should be the days when decisions were made by a select group of individuals who all looked alike, and whose opinions were accepted without question. Embracing diversity will help you become more productive and more successful. We still have work to do in this area.

One of the most productive and successful work groups I have ever been a part of was also the most diverse. Soon after arriving as an outside chief in Columbia, South Carolina, I recognized that the organization I was hired to lead lacked focus. They seemed to suffer from minimal convergence or direction. This was not their fault. They had been without a chief, other than an interim, for almost three years, and everyone in the organization seemed to be on a different path. The result was that they lacked a vision for the future.

These were good people who were competent at handling day-to-day operational issues and calls for service. They were more than capable and competent of solving everything from minor operational issues to complex crimes. However, it became very obvious to me that because of the lack of unity and direction, the organizational effectiveness was suffering.

Based on the experience I had with strategic planning in my former chief position in Greer, I formed what we called the strategic management and planning team (SMPT). The goals were to identify and address organizational shortcomings, and to create a strategic plan for the future. I opened up membership in the SMPT to anyone in the police department who wished to join. The only requirement was a commitment to excellence and a willingness to work as part of a dynamic team.

I was met with some resistance from some of the command staff. They thought it was a waste of time and resources, and they were certain that voluntary participation would be minimal. One of my majors even said, "Chief, don't get your hopes up that this proposed planning team is going to be met with much enthusiasm. I will be surprised if more than two or three people volunteer."

I replied, "I hope you are wrong, Major. For the sake of the entire department and our future, I sure hope I'm right."

To the major's surprise, and my delight, more than thirty-five employees signed on to be a part of the SMPT, which reflected approximately 10 percent of the workforce. Even better, the volunteers represented a meaningful cross-section of the police department, from all assignments, ranks, and tenure. They also represented every ethnicity and culture we had, and both men and women signed up. Overall, it was clear to me that we had a lot of employees who craved for participation in the guidance, future direction, and cohesion of the police department.

Because of the large number of volunteers, we had to limit the number of individuals we could accept. Too many people would have made it difficult for everyone to be heard, and would have delayed progress for the entire working group. This exuberant outpouring of volunteers was a terrific problem to have, especially since one of my majors had predicted that the only way to get people involved in strategic planning would be to draft individuals to serve.

I selected individuals primarily based on work assignment, years of service, recommendations from supervisors, and willingness to work as a dynamic team. I also considered gender and race because I wanted to make sure that all of our employees had a representative voice on the committee, and I knew it would be important to have a diverse cross-section of our department not only to formulate ideas, but because I needed everyone's acceptance of the recommendations and strategies we would reach.

After six months, the SMPT produced one of the most comprehensive and complete evaluations that our police organization had ever produced. In fact, the quality of our conversations and collaborations were inspirational. The problems we solved and the goals we set were critical to our achievements not only as a committee, but also as an entire police department.

Also, the ancillary benefits were numerous. We developed a comprehensive plan that gave us direction in the key areas of leadership, employee benefits, training, and community partnerships. The influence of the SMPT cultivated an atmosphere of teamwork, ownership, and leadership at all levels of the organization.

Personally speaking, the SMPT was incredibly helpful in keeping me well-informed of my employees' ideas and priorities. Without a doubt, one of the principal reasons for the success of the SMPT was its diversity, and from it, I learned a lesson I will carry with me for life.

Tips for Embracing Diversity

- Have an open mind.
- Recognize that you will have implicit biases.
- Eliminate glass ceilings.
- Inclusion and giving people a equal voice are keys to diversity.
- Don't listen to the naysayers.
- Understand that diversity is not a choice. It is a mandate.
- Communicate your personal support for diversity.

CHAPTER 34

GENCHI GENBUTSU

*Many spiritual teachers—in Buddhism, in Islam—
have talked about firsthand experience of the world as an
important part of the path to wisdom, to enlightenment.*

—Bell Hooks

Go see it, and see for yourself why you shouldn't go see it.

—Samuel Goldwyn

Genchi Genbutsu. When I first heard these words, I said, "Huh? What did you say?"

These Japanese words mean *Go and see for yourself.*

This maxim was recently used by one of the largest car manufacturers in the world, Toyota Motor Corporation. During 2011 and 2012, Toyota was forced to recall several million vehicles for repairs. The most notorious problem was an accelerator that stuck, sometimes at full acceleration, causing a few accidents and several near misses. This recall, and the events that led up to it, undermined Toyota's renowned reputation for quality and passenger safety.

The embattled leader of Toyota, Mr. Akio Toyoda, watched his company's image and financial future teeter on the verge of disaster. He knew that once the public lost faith in them, Toyota would lose market share and investors. Damage caused in a few weeks could cost the company its profits and reputation for years.

Beyond the business reasons, Mr. Toyoda felt great personal pain over this series of events.

During this time, Mr. Toyoda was criticized for his management style. Toyota employees claimed that he was isolated from the rank and file, and rumor had it that Mr. Toyoda listened only to his most trusted advisors. The result, the employees claimed, was an information filtration system that only allowed Mr. Toyoda to hear good news. No one—not even his inner circle advisors—wanted to be the bearer of bad tidings, so they painted every turn of events in the most positive light possible.

Fortunately, Mr. Toyoda remembered the *genchi genbutsu* philosophy, in the nick of time. Mr. Toyoda realized he needed some accurate answers, and he needed them immediately. He decided to go to the front lines, where employees were working on the accelerators and other parts. He met with the employees, saw the parts in production, learned the specifics of the problems, and made the appropriate corrections. Armed with frontline information, Mr. Toyoda pulled out all the stops to fix some engineering flaws and to institute rigorous quality control. He knew that if he could fix the mechanical problems quickly, he would have a fighting chance to repair the company's reputation in short order.

Mr. Toyoda realized that covering up the problem, or hoping it would resolve itself in due time, were both certain recipes for disaster. So he acted upon what he had learned directly from the front lines of production. Once he understood and corrected the problems, Mr. Toyoda was able to tell his marketing staff and the world, with a clear conscience, that he understood the shortcomings, and that the problems had been fully repaired.

And they have. Once again, Toyota vehicles are trusted and are selling in record numbers. *Genchi genbutsu* worked for Mr. Akio Toyoda, and for his entire corporation. Knowing about the situation firsthand allowed a talented leader to address not only the concerns of the public, but also restored the faith in his management amongst all his frontline employees.

As a leader, I have also encountered this type of situation. During my tenure as a chief, I have sometimes been guilty of listening only to the voices of those closest to me. Whether it was a homicide scene, a bank robbery, or an administrative snafu, I would listen to a few people's interpretation of the events. The end result was almost always predictable—and never good. As a leader, you must recognize that people will always filter their versions of the story based on their agenda or understanding, which can create a disconnect for the leader.

The leader of the organization is ultimately responsible for everything. Unless we go see every major situation for ourselves, we will be forced to rely upon the interpretation of someone else. Even the people who are closest to us, who care for us, and would never intentionally do anything to harm us, may miss a detail or misperceive a fact. When that happens, we are left with an incomplete, and therefore, inaccurate view of the situation. We then make crucial leadership decisions based upon limited knowledge.

Each human has his or her perspective, shaped by our own experiences and environments. Because we have all grown up with different influences, we all see the world differently. When you are in a position of leadership, *genchi genbutsu* is critical to the success of your decisions.

Many of the most successful leaders in history understood this concept. Imagine what would have happened if Patton did not have a firsthand view of the troops as they raced way across Europe in the victorious Red Ball Express. Winston Churchill's advisors encouraged him to flee London and lead from a safe place in the countryside. But Churchill ignored their advice and stayed in the city, even when he was being targeted by bombing raids, both night and day. Mayor Giuliani stayed the course, front and center, during the aftermath of the attacks on the World Trade Center. He supported the first responders, met with the president and the public to rally the hunt for the perpetrators, and he attended funerals and memorials for the victims.

Most leaders will never be in positions of that magnitude, but we all make decisions under extreme circumstances. We can never make the best decisions unless we go and see for ourselves.

Genchi genbutsu will show you the way. Go see for yourself.

Tips to See for Yourself

- The information you get from others has been through their filters.
- Make it a priority to get out of your office environment and walk around.
- Recognize that everyone has value.
- No one will see through your eyes. Only you can.
- Nothing replaces the importance of an in-person visit.

CHAPTER 35

KEEP LEADERSHIP SIMPLE

Life is really simple,
but we insist on making it complicated.

—Confucius

Leadership is simple, just not easy.

—Dean Crisp

On a recent flight from Phoenix to Charlotte, I was contemplating the previous week I had spent teaching leadership. During that week, we'd had many dynamic conversations about how to improve leadership abilities, and how to increase effectiveness. Many of the students had relayed stories regarding their attempts to understand the complexities of leadership, and how to become a great leader. I remember that one student, when called upon, had a particularly difficult time defining leadership. As I began to canvass the room for definitions, I found that others experienced the same problem. With so many variations of the definition of leadership, we couldn't find one that was simple.

I realized that many people who were performing as leaders, and who should have had a clear understanding of leadership, couldn't define it. In response, I have created a simple definition of leadership: Actions or behaviors designed or expressed to motivate people towards a desired outcome. I have found that this definition helps me stay focused on keeping my leadership simple

A leader's actions will speak louder than their words. The behavior of the persons led will reflect the leader's actions, and will give insight as to what the leader really wants. Leaders give direction by either design or expression. *Design* refers to direct communication. *Expressed* refers to a non-direct communication, such as a nonverbal clue.

Motivation is the key to leadership. Leaders motivate people in predominantly two ways: inspiration and manipulation. Inspired employees are much more likely to be happy and successful. Manipulation is used to direct the employee by policy, rules, laws, punishment, or reward. This type of motivation is not bad, but it does not motivate the employee to do more than is required.

Keeping leadership simple will get the best results from your people.

Tips on How to Keep Leadership Simple

- When faced with complex issues, remember that simple is better.
- Break problems into small parts. Don't try to eat the entire elephant at one sitting.

CHAPTER 36

RESPECT POWER

A leader is best when people barely know he exists.
When his work is done, his aim fulfilled, they will say:
we did it ourselves.

—Lao Tzu

Abraham Lincoln once said, "Every man to some degree can handle adversity, but if you truly want to judge a man's true character, give him power."

Power is defined as the ability to persuade or influence others. Power used correctly gets things done. But conversely, the abuse of power can be destructive. Have you ever had a supervisor who abused their power and made your working conditions far more difficult than they needed to be? Good leaders use power as a supplement, not a replacement for motivation.

Lord Acton, the British historian, famously said, "Power tends to corrupt, and absolute power corrupts absolutely."

Power is used in many ways, and it is important to understand some of the more common forms of power.

Positional power is based on the position or rank. This is one of the more frequently used and abused forms of power. Using positional power may be effective at times, but can be destructive if it is used too much. As a leader, you can order any subordinate to do any task simply because you have a higher position in the organization. Positional power is effective in emergency situations where the boss has to take charge and order compliance. But leaders must be careful when using only positional power to motivate employees. This usually gets compliance, but not buy-in.

Personal power refers to character traits or qualities a leader possesses. No one would argue that Mother Teresa, Dr. Martin Luther King Jr., John F. Kennedy, or Bill Clinton have appealing character traits, and thus, became powerful. Examples of those traits are charisma, dedication, and kindness. This type of power is not limited to the affluent or to a chosen few. Everyone has characteristics that can be used to influence others. You can often see this kind of power displayed during political campaigns. Voters often choose candidates based on personality instead of competence.

Connection power relates to one's connection with people in high-ranking positions. In other words, *who you know*. I have worked with individuals who use other people's power to abuse subordinates. You might say they use power as a stick to hit other people over the head. I once worked with an individual who was promoted through the ranks because of his friendship with the boss. And when this individual became the boss, he still needed the power of the more powerful boss to get things done. He would often begin meetings with phrases like, "The boss said..." In fact, nearly every time he tried to influence others, he would open his directions with the said phrase. Although he may have thought he was using power correctly, everyone realized that he could never stand on his own two feet. We knew that without his connection to the real boss, this leader had no legitimate power.

Expert power is garnered from what you know. The more one knows about a particular subject, or the more technical skill one possesses, the greater his power to influence others. Prior to September 11, 2001, no one was listening to experts on terrorism. They had little, or no, useful input in decisions, even within the law enforcement community. After the 9/11 attacks, anyone with terrorism expertise suddenly became a valued member of the community. After that one fateful day, we all were seeking terrorism advice.

Appropriate use of power is one of the best tools a leader can possess. Power should not be used to unduly to influence others to provide special benefits for the leader. Leaders have to be careful on how they use power, and the negative consequences for improper usage. Power should be respected and should be used as a benefit to the organization and the overall mission.

Tips for Respecting Power

- Power can be addicting. Be careful of how you use it.
- Power in small doses usually gets results.
- Avoid using power to take advantage of people.
- Consider the viewpoint of others on how you are using your power.
- Never use power for personal gain—that gain will always be short-term

CHAPTER 37

JUST DO IT

This life is for us to discover the divine within.
And that's really the key to life in many ways for me.
And the thing is, it's not for us to reason
why everything is what it is...
just do it.

—Jon Anderson

No, this is not a Nike commercial. While working patrol as a young police officer, I was training a rookie officer on the night shift. It was Sunday, and we were enjoying the quiet evening. At about midnight, the radio silence was broken by a faint voice on the radio. Because of the way the voice came in, I instantly recognized something was wrong.

As a cop, one of skills you try to develop quickly is the ability to decipher the radio talk. Most cops who have worked the road can decipher voice inflections and instantly determine the seriousness of the dispatched call. We can also discern the type of situation that other officers may be in, and get a sixth sense about when we need to respond, even before anyone asks for help.

With that in mind, I and the rookie started rolling toward where quiet officer had last been dispatched. Seconds after the first call, another call came from the same officer. This time, I recognized the voice as Charles, a friend and partner on my shift. Now there was no doubt he was in dire straits. Charles's voice was loud and clear. He broadcast that shots had been fired, and that he had been hit. The injured officer shouted out his exact location, and we proceeded to help at full speed.

We were not far away, so my rookie partner and I were the first backup unit on the scene. I remember seeing Charles lying on the ground, bleeding, his body spread across a concrete street drain. As I approached him, I saw that Charles was still breathing, but in obvious pain.

I leaned over and said, "Are you okay?"

Not sure what I was thinking, or what response I was hoping to get. Hell no, Charles wasn't okay. He had just been shot!

The officer replied, "Go and get my wife."

As you can imagine, the scene was intense. Other cops started arriving, along with the ambulance. The injured officer managed to give us a description of the suspect who had shot him, and the manhunt began immediately.

Police officers do this often enough that there is order to the chaos, but it is chaotic, nonetheless, due to fear that Charles would die; anger at the guy who had shot him; curiosity about what exactly had occurred; multiple hypotheses about where the suspect might be now; and a range of other emotions which reminded each officer that on any given day, the same thing could happen to us.

In a few moments, just as the ambulance was loading up the injured cop, I spoke briefly with the shift lieutenant. I told him that Charles had made a specific request for me to go get his wife. I told him that I had met Charles's wife, Teresa, a few times before. The lieutenant agreed that, to fulfill what might be this officer's last request, I should the pick his wife up and take her to the hospital. Cell phones were not in use at this time, so the ability to just pick up a phone and call her house was not an option. Besides, this was not the sort of news I would want to communicate by phone, and I certainly did not want Teresa to drive to the hospital in a panicked emotional state. One serious injury in the family was enough for that night.

I yelled at the rookie to get in our car, and we proceeded to the officer's home. It was now well after midnight. As you can imagine, the officer's wife, Teresa, had to work the next day, so she was sound asleep. As I approached the front door, I gathered my thoughts and tried to focus on what I was going to say. I had no formal training in crisis notification, so I was winging it. The rookie officer walked with me up toward the front door.

As we approached, I said, "Let me do the talking."

We rang the doorbell and got no response. As I began to ring the doorbell again, I saw a light turn on inside. Through a frosted glass pane inset in the front door, I could see Teresa shuffling toward the door. She peered out the opaque glass pane and saw the two of us, in uniform, standing on the porch. She hurried to open the door, and was now on high alert.

She screamed, "Oh, my God!"

I moved toward her and put my hand on her shoulder.

"Teresa, Charles has been shot," I whispered.

The wife screamed and took off running through the house. I and the rookie officer chased her. It looked more like a foot pursuit than a notification.

As we ran after her, I shouted, "Teresa, stop! He has only been shot a little bit."

She halted, wheeled around and stared at me. "What the hell does that mean?"

Realizing what a stupid thing I had said, I tried to think quickly again.

Although I didn't know how seriously he had been wounded, I wound up saying, "Charles is going to be okay. I spoke with him at the scene. He is breathing fine and talking, and he asked for you. The ambulance is already treating him, and they are taking him to the hospital. He just wants you to be there at the hospital with him so you know firsthand what is going on."

Teresa collapsed into a nearby chair and started to cry. After a few moments, she gathered herself, and we took her to the hospital. Upon arrival, we were notified that the injuries to Charles were indeed not life threatening. After a few months, he made a complete recovery and returned to work.

Although I was unprepared to deliver the bad news to Teresa, I knew that I had to *just do it*. Leadership can sometimes be like this. You are going to do things and make decisions for which you are not prepared. You just have to do it.

Colin Powell states that he never makes a decision on all the facts. He makes decisions on probabilities of success. In *It Worked For Me: In Life and Leadership*, he says, "Use the formula P equals forty to seventy, in which P stands for the probability of success, and the numbers indicate the percentage of information acquired." Then, "once the information is in the forty to seventy range, go with your gut."

What General Powell is saying is that sometimes you don't need all the information to make a good decision, or to *just do it*. Of course, information is a key factor in any decision, but sometimes your gut will guide you on what to do.

Hesitation can be the enemy of success. Today, excessive delays in the name of information-gathering breeds analysis paralysis. Procrastination in the name of reducing risk actually increases risk.

Sometimes you just have to do it.

Tips for Just Doing It

- Don't let fear keep you from moving forward.
- Have confidence in yourself.
- Use experience as a guide.
- Muster inner strength to support your decision.

CHAPTER 38

FIND THE RIGHT FIT

Fitting in is boring.
But it takes you nearly your whole life to work that out.

—Clare Balding

Organizations are like shoes in that they come in all sizes. And the decision to move from one organization to another, or to move within your own organization, can be difficult. People who desire to be promoted are sometimes faced with having to change assignments or to take on new responsibilities. This can be an exciting time, but also challenging. Many factors have to be considered before accepting the promotion or initiating the move. Two of those factors, frequently overlooked, are simple but profound: Are you a good fit with the new position?, and, How well does the new assignment or location fit you? Just like a new pair of shoes, moving into a new job location can be painful, and if it doesn't fit, can be hard to get out of.

Shortly after accepting a new position as a chief of police in a larger organization, I understood how important it is to be a good fit. I had been contemplating a move for several years, to accept a position in a larger department. I had been involved in a few police chief searches, and had been selected in the top three in all of them. I had even turned one offer down because I was concerned about the effects such a move would have had on my family. After my children had completed high school, I eventually found the organization that I believed would give me the right balance of challenge and opportunity.

The organization was and still is a good one, with many talented people and great potential. But I struggled with fitting in. Despite my best efforts to make the fit right, I was never able to settle in and get momentum in the right direction. I left as chief after three and a half years. To this day, I wish it would have worked better for me, and especially for the employees. They deserved better.

I learned a valuable lesson about making sure you are the right person at the right time for such an important leadership position. I initially underestimated the importance of a good fit. I was ready to move forward and make the sweeping changes I thought were needed. But the city manager, who was the former chief of police, did not see it that way. Although prior to me taking the job, we had discussed many needed changes, when it came time to implement them, he would offer limited support. This caused much consternation for everyone, and frustration for me. His style of change management was much slower than mine, which caused many problems. Although I have a great deal of respect for him, our differences regarding a sense of urgency did not make for a good fit.

This is a cautionary tale for anyone contemplating a job change. Make sure your leadership beliefs are in line with your boss.

A good fit requires a number of things to work for a good outcome:

You and the people within the organization must share the same values.

1. You must be able to adapt to the organization's culture.

2. You must have keep an open mind.

3. Timing is important. Make sure you are ready for the move, not just jumping a great opportunity.

4. If you sense that you do not have these things, or the support system, to make them situation work, then reevaluate your decision.

When you move into a new position, many variables are at work, and these factors can overwhelm even your best efforts. For example, if you are a hard charger and your leadership style is one of moving fast and furious, but you take over a unit that does not want change, you may be doomed from the start. The harder you push, the more resistance you will encounter. There may be a politician, or a CEO, or some other influential person, who wanted their child to get the job, but that VIP got outvoted or outmaneuvered, and you got the job instead. In this type of situation, even if you turn water to wine, it may not meet the expectations of that important stakeholder. Sometimes being a hard fit may be as simple as being the outsider in a place that prefers homegrown people.

Another mistake people who get promoted find is that relationships with employees are different. When you work with a certain group of people for any length of time, you develop relationships, and when you leave that group, you do not take those relationships with you. Unfortunately, we sometimes don't change our behavior to match the newness of the different relationship. We bring the same mannerisms and familiarity with us that we had in the old job because we are comfortable with them. But the new people we are now working with do not know us, and they are naturally guarded. Thus, they do not feel comfortable. Our behaviors aren't compatible, and we encounter resistance. If you do not work to develop relationships in every new job, the fit becomes strained.

Whatever the reason, I recommend you do as much homework as possible before accepting a promotion. Take an in-depth look from every angle. Visualize yourself in the position and working with the new responsibilities, understanding that you must take an honest look at yourself.

Are you ready for the new challenges ahead? While your education, experience, and qualifications all matter, you also need to evaluate the influence of political and social factors. They may not seem job-related to you, but to someone else they are the only things that matter. The ancillary issues that make up your *fit* with the position are vital. A good fit or a poor fit will significantly determine your success much more so than the best efforts and talent you devote to your job.

Tips for Finding the Right Fit

- Be clear on what you want out of a promotion.
- Decide your endgame, and how the move gets you closer to it.
- Do your homework
- Create a checklist of pros and cons of the move.
- Don't get caught up in believing the grass is greener somewhere else.

FINAL THOUGHTS

My hope is that this book has provided you with information that will make your leadership journey both positive and productive. After many years of experience and reflection, I now understand that leadership is the responsibility of everyone. We are all leaders in some areas of our lives.

When we begin to lead others, it becomes apparent how our knowledge and skills impact not only our lives, but the lives of others. Never forget how influential leaders can be, and how much of an impact they can have on others.

Leaders leave an indelible mark on who we are and who we become. Leading someone and trying to make their life better is a heavy responsibility and should not be taken lightly.

We have all been influenced by leaders. Unfortunately, we tend to remember the bad ones before the excellent ones. That is because we see damage before we recognize beauty.

Some Things to Remember

- Leadership begins with a partnership, is continued through relationships, and will ultimately produce synergy.
- Leadership is a lifestyle.
- As a leader, passion is a must.
- Are you all in? If not, those you lead will know, and you will not be effective.

- Your mindset is the number one factor in becoming a great leader, and should guide you every minute of every day.
- Having a mission for your life will give you direction and meaning, which will make you a stronger leader.
- Promises matter. Over-promise and under-deliver.
  /Under/ /Over/
- Every interaction with an employee matters.
- Being committed is more than just talking. It is also following through with actions.
- You must be willing to pay the price to accomplish anything great.
- Courage is not being unafraid. It is being afraid and doing it anyway.
- Self-confidence is a must if you are going to withstand all you will face as a leader.
- Before you know where you are going, you must first understand where you are. Having a GPS moment is crucial to the start of every journey.
- Trust your instincts.
- Goals without a strategies are only wishes.
- People do not care how smart you are, or how talented you are, until they know how much you care about them.
- Sacrifice is key to leadership, and can lead to service or suffering.
- Life is full of beauty. Appreciate it. Don't be in a hurry to *nowhere.*
- Mentoring others is the key to your personal success. Others matter.
- Lack of vision will lead to a constant state of wandering.
- Always do the right thing, for the right reason, at the right time, and in the right way.

- Growing future leaders is the number one job of every leader.

- Working trust is a must.

- Listening is mandatory.

- Anger and grudges are destructive. Don't let them control you.

- Diversity is not about a rainbow group of individuals. It is about giving everyone an equal voice.

- Janitors may not only have the keys to the building, they may be the key to the building. Don't overlook the people doing the grunge work.

- Leaders must be readers. Reading is a way to open your mind to new experiences.

- Don't just rely on the words of others. Go see for yourself.

- Leadership is simple—it's about people. In order to see others, you must first see yourself in them.

- Power is not for everyone.

- Live everyday forward. You can't do this if you are constantly looking in the rearview mirror.

- If your *yes* is more determined than their *no*, you will succeed.

- Sometimes you have to just do it.

- Make sure you're the right fit for the job.

- Empathy is the fastest form of human interaction. We can't live without it.

EPILOGUE

When preparing this book, I wanted to address some of the many questions I received from readers of my first book, *Leadership Lessons*, such as, *Was it difficult to write the book?* and *What are additional lessons you've learned since then?*

The opportunity to address these are in the following interview, where I sat down with Kelle Corvin, Director of Business Development for the Leaders Helping Leaders Network, to discuss some of these and other questions, as well as lessons learned. Many have become clearer and will be addressed in greater detail in my next book. Most of the lessons I have learned have been due to self-reflection, and gave me clarity as to my purpose going forward.

Although I've been a teacher of leadership for more than a decade now, my desire to grow future leaders has become more profound. If I can leave a legacy of leadership lessons to help a future *me* avoid some of the mistakes I've made along the journey, then my life's purpose has been fulfilled. My goal is to leave a leadership legacy that lives on in the lives of all those I have touched.

INTERVIEW WITH DEAN

DEAN CRISP: LESSONS LEARNED SINCE THE FIRST BOOK

Your first book, *Leadership Lessons* was published in 2017. Since then, you've been doing a lot of things. But let's start at the beginning. What made you want to write a book in the first place?

> Dean: Well, it was a way of conveying my experiences as a cop, a leader, a parent, and sharing them with others. I wrote the book because I'm like every other cop out there who has learned from his experiences. You just can't make the stories up, and I knew I wanted to write a book.
>
> Writing for me has always been a difficult task. As I tell people, I wasn't a great student in high school, and I had to put forth considerable, determined effort to get into and through community college, then college, and then graduate school. I knew that writing would not come easy, and in many ways, I think my journaling came from my desire and determination to get better as a reader and a writer. Initially, I used the journals to write down my thoughts on books I was reading. But it rapidly became a great way to catalog my leadership experiences.

The journaling started early on, when I was a corporal, then continued when I was sergeant, and on up to major, and then chief at thirty-three years of age. It was how I taught myself to reflect, which is something I didn't know was important. So, the twenty-five-plus years of journaling those experiences was a good foundation for me to take one lesson at a time and just start writing on it. I encourage all of my students and mentees to embrace this concept and use it as a way to organize their leadership and their thoughts. It was perhaps the single best way for me to look back and see how I had made decisions, why I had made them, and to reflect on whether they were correct. Without writing them down, it wouldn't have worked well, and I'm not sure I would have gotten the book written.

I was fortunate enough to have the foresight to start journaling my experiences on the job, and through leadership trials, which summarized the events I went through and the lessons learned as to what worked and didn't work. So, the book became an outcrop of those twenty-five-years-worth of journals. Those stories became the lessons that I wanted to share with others, especially those who were younger, so maybe my lessons would help them to avoid the mistakes I made.

You often say to your classes that the day you stop growing is the day you will die. Share with us some things you have learned since writing the book?

Dean: For sure, that is so true! I'll tell you that as a leader, you are leaving a legacy every day, and you had better be aware of what that legacy is. Continuous personal growth will always lead to continuous growth of the leader. Definitely, there is no doubt that you always learn more after you write the book. The acceptance and response I received from law enforcement regarding the book was really amazing.

All of the things the profession has experienced since 2008 has caused many of the men and women in blue to lose sight of their *brotherhood*. In all of the classes I teach, I notice that there was a desire to have more connection with other law enforcement officers for both learning and comradery. To that end, I have created the Leaders Helping Leaders Network to provide a way for leaders to connect, to mentor, and learn from other professionals. My goal in creating LHLN was to give my students what they wanted, which was to continue their learning after the class, and to advance to the next level of leadership.

How long did it take you to write and publish the book?

Dean: It took a lifetime of experiences to write it, but not a lifetime to put it together. As a project, I would say it was about five years of focus to put it together.

Now remember, as I said earlier, my writing skills were not great. Writing doesn't come easy for me, and never has. I write how I talk, which sometimes doesn't translate into a grammatically correct work. I wanted the first book to be a recollection of my life experiences and lessons. My guess is that if I were to do a similar project today—and I am working on a couple—it would take me about a year.

What was the biggest transformation you experienced both personally and professionally from writing the book?

Dean: I am typically a private person. I don't share a lot with anyone. Even sharing the stories behind the lessons in the book was a big step for me. But I knew that by sharing those lessons, I would either help someone else avoid the mistakes I had made, or encourage them to make the right decision in a difficult circumstance.

One of the biggest professional transformations for me has been hearing the many thanks from all over the country and world, in regard to how the book helped them. That is tremendously reaffirming that you did the right thing. I am motivated to help others become the best version of themselves. As a nationally known speaker and teacher, if letting people gain a better understanding of who I am and what has motivated me to learn and grow, helps them grow, then that is transformational not only for me, but for them as well.

The book did transform me by making me take a closer look at my career to see how these lessons had impacted my own philosophy of leadership. It led me to create a new class called Intentional Leadership, where I teach about the four pillars of leadership. One of those pillars is self-reflection, which was a direct result of writing the book. Seeing how people reacted to the book also transformed me because it encouraged me to take my leadership as an instructor more seriously. I now see the tremendous impact instructors have on their students. As a teacher, it made me see that I have great influence on helping my students become the best they can be.

You have to remember that in the era I became a cop—in the mid-1970s—and in the early days of leadership, leaders could say what they wanted to say. Most leadership—and in particular, law enforcement leadership—was extremely paternalistic. The attitude was, *Do as I say, not as I do.* Writing the book taught me that every encounter with the boss matters. Now, I believe every encounter with a student matters, and I am measured in everything I say.

Did the writing the book lead you to learn new lessons?

Dean: Oh, absolutely. One hundred percent. A lot of them will be in the next book, *The Leadership Recipe.* As a sneak peak, two of the biggest that come to mind are the importance of self-reflection and how I lead others. Honest self-reflection is what matters as a leader. It is the hardest thing to do, mainly because of cognitive dissonance, meaning that you will find a way to justify your decision, your action, your leadership. That has greatly impacted the way I lead others, both professionally and personally.

Another lesson learned—which was a *kaboom!* moment—is that we all fall into one of three levels of motivation in anything we do. The first is, you *kinda wanna* do it. Meaning that you know there are benefits to doing it, but you don't have that higher motivation to do it. A good example of this would be to *kinda wanna* workout. You know that you'll probably feel better and maybe lose weight, but you don't have the drive to do it consistently.

The second level of motivation is being *determined* to do it now. When you are determined to do it, you will work it into your schedule like you would a meeting, and it becomes part of your routine.

The third level is being *driven* to get it done. At this level, you will do whatever it takes to make sure it gets accomplished. One of the stories I show in my class is a video on David Goggins. Goggins is one of these iconic figures who was a mess at one point in his life—his words, not mine. He was driven to become a US Marine, and worked so hard at it that he was willing to go through the proving ground not once, not twice, but three times. To this day, the man is one of the most inspirational people you will follow, however, his social media posts are NOT for the "G-rated" crowd.

Which chapter or lesson was the most difficult one for you to learn?

Dean: Hands down, it was *empathy*. In fact, I'm sure I'm still learning it to this day. You see again, cops of my era were taught to compartmentalize the job— to see everything as a linear action. When you view things linearly, you tend to see every person, every problem as a thing to fix or deal with. As I started to learn about holistic thinking and how to see all people and things as parts of the whole, I started to become a more empathetic person.

I learned that the more empathetic you are, the more humble you are. The more humility you exhibit, the more you get back from your people. Maybe the best quote comes from former San Francisco 49ers wide receiver Jerry Rice. He said, "I will do today what others won't do, so that tomorrow I will do what others can't do."

I'll give you a great personal example of how empathy has grown in my life. I was a cop at all levels for more than thirty-seven years. In that time, I was out for physical reasons maybe three times? Now I am thankful that I've always been blessed with excellent health. But think about how that likely impacted my ability to show empathy to coworkers or employees. Part of it was the work ethic I had learned from my mother. But I also held the view that you didn't stay home if you had the sniffles. Noble in the day, but you can only imagine how that informed my view of employees who were constantly out sick, or had a chronic illness that caused them recurring health problems. My lack of empathy toward their personal circumstances created a negative view of my employees at times, and a jaded view of my workforce. Were they just lazy? Did they not want to work? This viewpoint I held created lack of empathy for my employees.

You achieved a high level of success at a young age. What challenges and lessons did you learn from that?

Dean: First and foremost—and I mean this with all due respect to young leaders of which both you and I were—age is just an excuse. What is really going on is that leaders cannot have wisdom and youth at the same time. I am definitely a great example of this saying. In fact, one of the biggest mistakes that any leader—regardless of age—makes is to wait until they get better at a specific skill, such as empathy, before practicing it. That's what happened to me in many areas. But think about that for a minute. If you were a professional baseball player, you sure as heck aren't gonna wait until you get better at hitting home runs before you try. No, you practice it daily.

Sheriff Alfonzo Williams of Burke County, Georgia said it best: "You can't have youth and wisdom." I believe that is true. I lacked the wisdom on the importance of empathy and humility. So with young leaders, you often see too much enthusiasm and too little experience. Usually what happens is that the enthusiasm will inspire others to follow, and that's where you accomplish things. Regardless of my age, I never accomplished anything without the commitment and dedication of others.

What would you tell a new or young leader?

Dean: The first thing I would say is, *Get comfortable with being uncomfortable.* Being a leader is never a comfortable situation, and it is your job to be okay with that. The second thing I would say is to read my book! (Just kidding) However, I do hope that the lessons I share in my book allow others to avoid the mistakes I made as a leader.

When you are a leader, yes, you get to make decisions. But you also make a lot of uncomfortable decisions because you have to do so for the betterment of the entire organization. For the betterment of the morale of your people. We've seen this recently with the coronavirus shutdowns. The adjustments being made were unprecedented and uncomfortable. But leaders had to make the tough decisions for the greater good.

The second thing I would say is that you have to adjust your thinking. I talk about mindset constantly as the cornerstone of effective leadership. The old saying, *thoughts are things,* is true. If you have a cruddy mindset toward your job, your people, your organization, I can guarantee that you will end up with a cruddy experience with one or all of those parts. *Change your mindset, change your leadership* is my mantra.

The third thing I would say is to understand your *why* of leadership. Going back to the *kinda wanna, determine, driven* discussion earlier, if you don't know why you want to lead, or how your *why* of leadership ties to the organizational purpose, how in the world do you expect your people to follow you? Simon Sinek's book *Start With Why*, has had a profound effect on my view of this for leadership development.

The fourth thing I would say is to find your GPS Moment. You better know why you're doing it. But you also better know where you are and how you are going to get there as a leader. When people get promoted to a leadership position, many have shown functional excellence to their superiors. What I am suggesting is that you need to understand where you are now as a leader, and what you want your destination to be. It's the only way to grow yourself and others. As I always say, the rent you pay as a leader are the leaders you leave behind when you are gone.

If you do those four things, then you will likely get off to a good start. Never forget that your leadership success will be dependent on other people and how you grow them as leaders.

If you think about a commercial plane. The pilot is there to redirect the plan because—and I didn't know this for many years—99.9 percent of the time, it's off course! So, the pilot has to make the redirection to get you to your destination. Leadership is the same. Your people will be going in a million different directions, and it takes a focused, purpose-filled leader to redirect them to accomplish the organizational goals and objectives.

One of the epiphany moments for me is where you talk about leadership and the Diamond Leadership Model, which allows leaders to be the most effective they can be. How did that model come about?

Dean: Well, I think I said earlier that nothing I accomplished as a chief of police or a leader was done without people. My leadership got better when I realized that people were part of the success, not subservient to my leadership goals. The LRPS model came about when I was teaching one afternoon and talking about this fact to the class. You see, the synergy that is created in the classroom comes from, when you are an effective instructor, everyone wants to connect with each other. The teacher wants to connect with the student, and the student wants to connect with the teacher, as well as with the other students, and that's where the partnership is created. Why not help each other grow?

So I wrote on the board one day that Leadership = Relationship + Partnership. It was those three for a while. The fourth point, Synergy, came later from a conversation I had one night at dinner with Chief Todd Radford from Lakeway, Texas. He suggested that a fourth point be added. I took it under consideration, rethought the model, and said, "Yeah, it really does need the fourth point."

When a leader effectively creates a relationship with his people, a partnership is formed to achieve the organizational mission, which, in turn, creates synergy. Remember, synergy is another word for harmony. Each one has components that become a measurement of that component, as outlined in Chapter 28.

Since writing the book, what have you been up to?

Dean: Wow! So much, really. I am definitely much more serious about my own leadership and conveying a deeper level of understanding of how leaders are created and grown. I am committed to growing our LHLN business and the LHLN network so it can continue to grow leaders even after I'm long gone. Leadership is a growth process. Now that doesn't just mean rank, but growth as a person and as a leader.

I have also created three new live classes: *Intentional Leadership: Leading With a Purpose, Becoming a Character-Driven Officer, and a Master Presenter* class, out of the ideas I discussed in my first book. The class has helped me define, refine, and share the growth with others. Our team of instructors is always creating new classes designed to help law enforcement and other leaders adapt to a rapidly-changing environment. I've created my first eCourse and just conducted our first live, virtual class. These latter two really pushed me out of my comfort zone as an instructor, but that is what it's all about!

Speaking of your Intentional Leadership class, mentoring is a huge part of LHLN and the Thirty-Three-and-One-Third rule. You talk about that some in your first book. But why has that become so important to you?

Dean: As I say in the book, as a leader, the rent you pay are the leaders you grow.

Growth as a leader comes in three ways:

1. What you learn from others—those with more experience, as well as those at your level.

2. What you teach yourself by reading, taking classes, observing, and self-reflecting.

3. What you teach others.

I call this the One-Third rule, where you spend one-third of your time learning from others, one-third teaching yourself, and one-third teaching others. Remember, you are leaving a legacy every day. Your actions determine what that legacy will be.

One thing I've learned about the leaders I get to see and spend time with every week when I travel for teaching, is that there is tremendous desire to be as good a leader as they can be. But often, they don't have the maturity to be their best. I talk about this in my three levels of leadership. Most leaders will fall into one of these three categories of leadership: *survival, successful,* or *significant.* The least mature leader is a survival leader who is concerned strictly with surviving in their position as a leader. There is a *me* focus to all they do. The more mature leader is a successful leader. This is where many leaders stay for their entire career. They are concerned only with their people, their team. But the most mature leaders are those focused on being significant leaders. The significant leader is concerned about their people, their organization, and the impact they are making to transform people. What we hope they learn is to become a lifelong learner.

Personal growth is at the top of the significant leader's list of priorities. They seek to grow themselves, which automatically makes them want to grow others. If you stop growing, your organization will stop growing. Significant leaders will consistently display the three S's: sacrifice, service, and suffering. When a leader only focuses on their suffering, they are done. Life has become too comfortable.

So I know you wrote the book mostly for law enforcement. But the lessons are applicable outside of law enforcement, including as a parent. My life experience has taught me that parenting is leadership. Given that fact, is there anything you would you do differently as a parent?

Dean: When I dedicated the book to my family and my twin sons, it was because many of the lessons I learned were from parenting. Now, I will say that I wouldn't be less strict because I was determined to keep them alive. But I would be more humble and less competitive.

When you are a parent of multiples, it's a given that you can't have two good days in a row. One day, a great thing is happening to one of your kids. And the next, the other is experiencing failure. You rarely have your kids succeeding in sync or failing in sync. That definitely translates to leadership. As a leader, you will likely not have two good days in a row. Remember that in leadership or parenting. Be comfortable with being uncomfortable. Celebrate the good days, and mentor through the bad days. It's the best you can do as a parent, or as a significant leader.

There's no doubt that your first book *Leadership Lessons* was successful. What was the biggest surprise in becoming a published author?

Dean: Probably the biggest surprise—and I'm sure I'm not the only author that has said this—is that people actually wanted to buy the book, and took the time to read and rate it! It was humbling and rewarding. To think that what I had written mattered to anyone outside of my immediate circle of colleagues and friends was an incredible experience.

As a leader and a teacher, knowing that what you have written or taught made a difference in someone else's life is an indescribable experience.

In the process of publishing the book and signing a contract, it was like all of sudden I had a staff of six people working on the book. I learned a lot about the publishing process, though. It taught me that I have to be determined and know that there will be roadblocks along the way. But as I've always told my sons, your determination has to be stronger than roadblocks you encounter.

Do you have new books planned?

Dean: Definitely! Over the next twelve to eighteen months, we will be publishing three books. The next book I'm writing will be totally different from the first two. It's written as more of a leadership allegory that walks a new supervisor through a recipe for leadership success, from his mentor. Please know that my desire to write isn't about me. It's about sharing what ideas with others to help them grow. My goal is to share what I have learned, and continue to learn more about leadership. My *why* statement is simple:

To provide the information, inspiration, and instruction that leads others to find and live a purpose-driven life.

Whether they are in law enforcement, or not in a leadership role at all, I want to help as many people become the best version of themselves. You see, in my way of viewing others, everyone is a leader— from the stay-at-home mom who manages daily routines and monitors homework, to the leader of the free world—every single one of us is a leader of something. My goal is to share my knowledge in a way that will allow everyone to understand how to become the best version of themselves.

So let's finish up with some advice to new or current leaders. What would be the top three things you would tell them to focus on to be successful?

Dean: Well, I've been reading a book called, and they talk about a few things that echo what my advice would be:

- Believe you can make it happen. In other words, be driven.

- Form habits that are in line with the direction you want to go. Habits come from consistently performing the actions you wish to develop.

- Know where you are going, and refine that direction every day by developing a plan of action to develop the characteristics you want to exhibit.

I always use exercise, or physical fitness, as an example of this. If you believe you can run a marathon, if you develop the necessary habits to train for that marathon, if you are aware that you will face setbacks and are prepared to make adjustments to overcome those setbacks during the marathon training, you will be successful in achieving your goals. In leadership, as in life, the destination is not absolute. It is constantly changing.

What's at least one lesson you want readers of this book to take away?

Dean: Well, there are many, actually. But if I had to choose just one lesson...I think that it would be this: If I can do it, I know you can do it. If I can push myself from extremely humble beginnings, then you can achieve the success you desire. Your determination and willingness to pay the price to succeed will be the difference. Remember, don't ever judge your success by comparing yourself to others. Always try to be the best version of yourself.

You'll find that you will surprise others, and yourself, by doing just that.

ACKNOWLEDGMENTS

There are many people to thank for this project, especially those folks who served as examples within the book, while teaching me the important components of leadership. There are also those who have agreed to read and provide guidance along my journey of writing this book, and I am deeply indebted and will be forever grateful.

Thank you to Tim Plotts, a retired captain of the North Carolina State Highway Patrol, who I consider to be a brother. He has spent countless hours listening to my ideas and concepts about the book. And thanks to Kathleen Sheehan, a former LAPD lieutenant and chief of police, for her help in editing and reading the manuscript.

I also thank and recognize the contributions of Tom Stone, former chief of police and executive director of the FBI-LEED; Donna Carpenter, director of training for FBI-LEEDA; Skip Robb, former FBI agent and current director of FBI-LEEDA; fellow instructors in FBI-LEEDA: David Allen, Jennifer Harris, Neil Moore, Jerry Thompson, Todd Radford, Ron Bayne, Jon Felhman, Terry Wilfong, and Anne Kirkpatrick.

I was fortunate to have several former employees, colleagues, and leaders who believed in me and helped me through some tough leadership challenges, and I am forever grateful. They are as follows: Captain Jolene Vancil, Captain Buddy Dodson, Sergeant Mike Modica, Sergeant Florence McCants, Captain George Drafts, Debbie Collum, Mack Marsh, Jimmy Auld,

Vandell McCrary, Sergeant Chris Butzer, Scott Southern, Tammy Duncan, Jeff Smith, Barbara Greer, Mary Greer, Lannie Durham, Mark Cleveland, City Administrator Ken Westmoreland, City Administrator Ed Driggers, and City Manager Charlie Austin.

I am also thankful for the many elected officials I worked for, including Mayor Don Wall, Mayor Shirley Rollins, Mayor Bob Coble, and Mayor Rick Danner.

Thank you to the individuals who were significant in my growth when I began my teaching career: Lynda Leventis-Wells (a Greenville County School Board member) and B.J. Nash, who continues to offer her media expertise and support to this day.

Thank you to the members of the Greer Police Department SRT Team (VIKINGS): Lieutenant Roy Wright, Sergeant Hobart Lewis (now Sheriff of Greenville County, South Carolina), Sergeant Randle Ballenger Mixon Eldridge, Marc Ford, Dale Arterburn, Cindy Holiday, Perry Bowens, Shane Plemmons Adolph Ramos, Dr. Karl Kelley. Motto: 100% Heart, 100% Effort, 100% Voluntary.

I would also like to thank some of the police officers I worked with early in my career. They helped mold me into the person I have become. In particular, I want to thank Jon Kirkpatrick, who became my best friend out of rookie school; Carolyn Greene and Barbara Wolfe, who were cadets with me; and Gene Jarvis, who was my first rookie school teacher. Thanks also to Mike Berry, Will Annarino, Ross Robinson, Ted Lambert, Van Smith, Walt Robertson, Don Babb, Lee Carver, Dave Bossard, Mike Calloway, Lee Banks, Lee Warren, and James Ratcliff.

I know I will forget to mention some worthy people, and I apologize. There are so many people who touch us without knowing, and whom we touch without knowing.

I also want to thank my mom, who is now deceased. She taught me my work ethic and commitment, and to always stay focused on my goals. I thank my dad for our relationship and his support. And his wife Wanda. Thank you to my sister, Janet, who provided unselfish and dedicated support of our mom, and who has always been there for me. And thanks to Ricky Allen for taking care of my mom and sister, Janet. Also, thank you Gary O'Shields for being my best friend for over thirty-five years. And thanks to his partner-in-life, Loretta.

Most importantly, thanks to my wife, Kim; our sons, Adam and Andrew; our beautiful daughters-in-law, Morgan and Ashley; and all of our sweet, sweet grandchildren: Addie, Parker, Josey, Ada, Miller, and Beckham. Your support as I worked through this process of writing and publishing has been invaluable.

Special Thanks

I would like to give a special shout-out and thanks to Kelle Corvin, Business Development Director for the Leaders Helping Leaders Network, for her hard work and dedication in getting *Essential Leadership Lessons from the Thin Blue Line* published. She not only helped find a new, great publisher in Light Messages, but she worked tirelessly to assist with the edits throughout the process and make this a truly exceptional leadership book. Without her help, this would not have happened.

BIBLIOGRAPHY

Burns, James MacGregor. *Transforming Leadership*. Grove Press. New York, 2003.

Powell, Colin. *It Worked for Me: In Life and Leadership*. Harper Perennial. New York, 2012.

Covey, Stephen R. *The 7 Habits of Highly Effective People: Powerful Lessons in Personal Change*. Simon and Schuster. New York, 1989.

Eze, Michael Onyebuchi. *Intellectual History in Contemporary South Africa*. Palgrave Macmillan. New York, 2010.

Frankl, Viktor E. *Man's Search for Meaning*. Beacon Press. Boston, Massachusetts, 1959.

Giuliani, Rudolph W. *Leadership*. Hyperion. New York, 2002.

Golman, Daniel, Richard Boyatzis, and Annie McKee. *Primal Leadership: Unleashing the Power of Emotional Intelligence*. Harvard Business Review Press. Boston, Massachusetts, 2013.

Johnson, Spencer. *Peaks and Valleys*. Atria Books. New York, 2009.

Maxwell, John C. *The 21 Irrefutable Laws of Leadership: Follow Them and People Will Follow You*. Thomas Nelson, Inc. Nashville, Tennessee, 2003.

Maxwell, John C. *The 360 Degree Leader: Developing Your Influence from Anywhere in the Organization*. Thomas Nelson, Inc. Nashville, Tennessee, 2005.

Phillips, Donald T. *Lincoln on Leadership: Executive Strategies for Tough Times*. Hachette Book Group. New York, 1992.

Shickler, Scott and Waller, Jeff. *The 7 Mindsets To Live Your Ultimate Life*. Next Century Publishing. Austin, Texas, 2011.

Sinek, Simon. *Start With Why: How Great Leaders Inspire Everyone to Take Action*. Penguin Books. New York, 2009.

Snair, Scott. West Point Leadership Lessons: Duty, Honor, and other Management Principles. Sourcebooks. Naperville, Illinois, 2005.

Sullenburger, Chesley B. and Zaslow, Jeffrey. *Highest Duty: My Search for What Really Matters*. Harper Collins. New York, 2009.

Brainy Quote, www.brainyquote.com.

The Free Dictionary, www.thefreedictioary.com.

READER RESOURCES

In several chapters, I referenced our Reader Resources, all designed to help you grow your leadership. To facilitate this for our readers, you can find all of the resources listed below, on our website, www.lhln.org. Be sure to bookmark that website, as we will add resources as we discover them from other sources, and develop them for our students and readers.

Join our Leaders Helping Leaders Network, where you can join in the conversation about this book and other leadership issues.

As a student and practitioner of leadership, I view my role as that of a partner. I want to hear from you! Please let me know your thoughts and feelings on this book, and the topics herein. Let me know if I can help you or your organization, by scheduling one of our classes, or asking me to speak as a keynote for a professional conference or meeting. My *why* is to inform, inspire, and instruct others to help them live a purpose-driven life.

Thank you for reading and sharing! As I always say, *Learn It, Live It,* and *Share It.*

Resources Available at www.lhln.org

- The Diamond Leadership Model Assessment
- About Being a Cop
- About Leading Law Enforcement
- Self-Assessments
- Mindset Check

- Behavior Style
- Values Exercise
- Motivators
- LHLN's process for developing your *why* of leadership
- Examples of Exemplary Organizational Vision Statements

LANDMARK BOOKS

From the extensive list of self-help and leadership books I have read, I share some of the best of the best. I believe it is important for anyone who is looking for a book to read to first evaluate your mindset in relation to leadership. Let me explain further. If you are a new leader and have not read deeply about leadership, you would have a different perspective from someone who has had years of experience and has read extensively. Suggesting a book full of many scientific theories and studies would be of little value to someone who is looking for an introductory level of leading. I have been selective in listing best-selling books that have genuine and helpful content. Books which have stood the test of time.

Below is a list of books I highly recommend:

The 7 Habits of Highly Effective People: Powerful Lessons in Personal Change by Stephen R. Covey

The 4 Disciplines of Execution: Achieving Your Wildly Important Goals by McChesney, Stephen R. Covey, and Jim Huling

Who Moved My Cheese by Spencer Johnson, MD

The One Minute Manager by Spencer Johnson, MD, and Kenneth Blanchard, PhD

Peaks and Valleys: Making Good and Bad Times Work for You – at Work and in Life by Spencer Johnson, MD

The Power of Positive Thinking by Norman Vincent Peale

The Leadership Challenge: How to Make Extraordinary Things Happen in Organizations by Kouzes and Posner

Lincoln on Leadership: Executive Strategies for Tough times by Donald T. Phillips

The Four Agreements: A Practical Guide to Personal Freedom by Don Miguel Ruiz

The 7 Mindsets To Live Your Ultimate Life: An Unexpected Blueprint for an Extraordinary Life by Scott Shickler and Jeff Waller

The 360 Degree Leader: Developing Your Influence from Anywhere in the Organization by John C. Maxwell

Talent Is Never Enough: Discover the Choices That Will Take You Beyond Your Talent by John C. Maxwell

The Founding Fathers on Leadership: Classic Teamwork in Changing Times by Donald T. Phillips

Good to Great: Why Some Companies Make the Leap... and Others Don't by Jim Collins

StrengthsFinder 2.0 by Tom Rath

Social Intelligence: The New Science of Human Relationships by Daniel Goleman

On Leadership by Harvard Business Review

Man's Search for Meaning by Viktor Frankl

Social: Why Our Brains are Wired to Connect by Michael D. Lieberman

Leadership by Rudy W. Giuliani

Start With Why: How Great Leaders Inspire Everyone to Take Action by Simon Sinek

Leaders Eat Last: Why Some Teams Pull Together and Others Don't by Simon Sinek

ABOUT THE AUTHOR

Dean Crisp is a thirty-eight-year veteran of law enforcement. During that time, he spent twenty-one years in a command leadership position. Quickly rising through the ranks of law enforcement, he was promoted to captain at the age of twenty-nine, major at thirty-one, and police chief at thirty-three. Dean served seventeen years as a police chief, and retired as the chief of police  in Columbia, South Carolina, in 2008, to pursue his passion of teaching. He joined FBI-LEEDA in 2009, and has been traveling extensively throughout the United States, teaching leadership to law enforcement professionals.

In 2018, Crisp started the Leaders Helping Leaders Network, dedicated to providing a way for leaders to connect with their leaders. He has created several new live classes and e-courses on leadership, which he continues to teach outside of FBI-LEEDA.

Dean has received numerous state and national awards, including the National Thomas Jefferson Award, at a young age, for establishing a summer camp program for at-risk youth in Asheville, North Carolina. He attended night school while working full-time, and earned three advanced degrees. Dean has an associate of arts degree in criminal justice, a bachelor's in criminal justice, and a master's in public affairs, also from Western Carolina University. He is also a graduate of the FBI-National Academy (session 172), FBI-LEEDA, and the United States Secret Service DPS. He also trained with the Israeli National Police.

Crisp is frequently asked to speak at national-level conferences and leadership seminars on such topics as executive leadership, motivating employees, and community policing. He has also presented a TEDxTryon where he introduced his concept of the Warrior-Guardian Model of 21st century policing.

Dean is married to his high school sweetheart, Kim, who is a registered nurse with Mission Hospital in Asheville, NC. They have twin sons, Adam and Andrew. Adam and his wife, Ashley, have two sets of twin daughters, Adeline, Parker, Ada and Josie. Andrew and his wife, Morgan, have fraternal twins, daughter, Miller, and son, Beckham.

Contact Dean:
hdcrisp@yahoo.com
803-240-3024

Follow Dean:
Facebook: Leaders Helping Leaders
Instagram: lhlncrisp
Twitter: @LHLN5
LinkedIn: Dean Crisp

Learn more about Dean and his publications:
www.DeanCrisp.com

Book Dean for a class or speaking engagement:
www.lhln.org/live-classes
kcorvin@lhln.org
864-275-4800